Create
Your Own
Website

Using What You Already Know

SCOTT MITCHELL

SAMS   800 East 96th Street, Indianapolis, Indiana 46240

Create Your Own Website
Using What You Already Know

International Standard Book Number: 0-672-32662-0

Library of Congress Catalog Card Number: 2004095060

Printed in the United States of America

First Printing: August 2004

07   06   05   04   4   3   2

Trademarks

Warning and Disclaimer

Bulk Sales

Sams Publishing offers excellent discounts on this book when ordered in quantity for bulk purchases or special sales. For more information, please contact

U.S. Corporate and Government Sales
1-800-382-3419
corpsales@pearsontechgroup.com

For sales outside of the U.S., please contact

International Sales
international@pearsoned.com

Associate Publisher
Michael Stephens

Acquisitions Editor
Neil Rowe

Development Editor
Mark Renfrow

Managing Editor
Charlotte Clapp

Project Editor
Andrew Beaster

Copy Editor
Benjamin Berg

Indexer
Erika Millen

Proofreader
Wendy Ott

Technical Editor
Doug Holland

Publishing Coordinator
Cindy Teeters

Multimedia Developer
Dan Scherf

Book Designer
Gary Adair

Contents at a Glance

Table of Contents

About the Author

Create Your Own Website Using What You Already Know is author **Scott Mitchell**'s sixth book, his others being *Sams Teach Yourself Active Server Pages 3.0 in 21 Days* (Sams); *Designing Active Server Pages* (O'Reilly); *ASP.NET: Tips, Tutorials, and Code* (Sams); *ASP.NET Data Web Controls Kick Start* (Sams); and *Teach Yourself ASP.NET in 24 Hours* (Sams). Scott has also written a number of magazine articles, including articles for Microsoft's *MSDN Magazine* and *asp.netPRO*, as well as hundreds of online articles on his website, 4GuysFromRolla.com.

Scott's non-writing accomplishments include speaking at numerous technical user groups and conferences across the country. Scott has also taught numerous web technology classes at the University of California—San Diego University Extension. In addition to teaching and writing, Scott also is a software developer. He works as an independent consultant and has authored and sold a number of commercial software applications.

Scott lives in San Diego, California with his wife, Jisun, and dog, Sam.

You can learn more about Scott at http://www.4GuysFromRolla.com/ScottMitchell.

Dedication

To my lovely and beautiful wife, Jisun.

We Want to Hear from You!

As the reader of this book, *you* are our most important critic and commentator. We value your opinion and want to know what we're doing right, what we could do better, what areas you'd like to see us publish in, and any other words of wisdom you're willing to pass our way.

As an associate publisher for Sams Publishing, I welcome your comments. You can email or write me directly to let me know what you did or didn't like about this book—as well as what we can do to make our books better.

Please note that I cannot help you with technical problems related to the topic of this book. We do have a User Services group, however, where I will forward specific technical questions related to the book.

When you write, please be sure to include this book's title and author as well as your name, email address, and phone number. I will carefully review your comments and share them with the author and editors who worked on the book.

Email: feedback@samspublishing.com

Mail: Michael Stephens
         Associate Publisher
         Sams Publishing
         800 East 96th Street
         Indianapolis, IN 46240 USA

For more information about this book or another Sams Publishing title, visit our website at www.samspublishing.com. Type the ISBN (0672326620) or the title of a book in the Search field to find the page you're looking for.

Welcome to
Create Your Own Website Using What You Already Know!

As the popularity of the Internet and the World Wide Web have risen over the past decade, virtually all businesses have established an online presence. Many individuals, too, have left their imprints on the web, creating a website for their family, or posting pictures of their vacations. If you want to join the millions of people who have created websites, but fear you lack the background or expertise for such an endeavor, this book is for you!

In this book you'll see just how easy creating a website can be. The CD included with this book contains five professional website templates and a free web page editor. With the web page editor you can quickly and easily customize the provided templates into your very own personal websites. Using the web page editor is as simple as using a word processor program. It's just point and click!

> *"If you want to join the millions of people who have created websites, but fear you lack the background or expertise for such an endeavor, this book is for you!"*

Since there are a number of different types of websites on the Internet, this book's CD includes five different templates for five differ-ent types of sites. Specifically, the five provided templates will let you quickly create the follow-ing types of sites:

1. **Family websites**—With a family website you can share pictures of you and your family with friends and members of your extended family.

2. **Hobby websites**—A hobby website allows you to share your hobbies with others who have similar interests.

3. **Community websites**—With a community website your church, club, bowling team, or other group or association can post schedules, pictures, and other pertinent information.

4. **Informational websites**—Share information about your business's products or services with a brochure-ware site.

5. **Online storefront websites**—Sell products online by accepting credit card payments with an online storefront site.

Along with step-by-step instructions for creating your own websites, this book also contains a number of website reviews. These reviews provide recommendatons, tips, and helpful hints that you can use to improve your own websites. The best way to learn, after all, is to examine the work of others!

Get ready to see just how fun and easy it is to create your very own websites!

Special thanks to Kim Spilker, Sams Product Marketing Manager, for contributing the website reviews.

CHAPTER 1

Creating Your First Web Page

Have you ever wanted to create your own website, but thought that the task was too daunting? Do you think that only folks with years of computer training and experience have the knowledge necessary for building web pages? These are common misconceptions that many people have. With the right tools and information, creating websites is as easy as pointing and clicking! If you are interested in quickly creating a professional-looking website, then you've picked up the right book.

> **NOTE**
>
> Don't have any website building experience? Don't worry! This book's CD contains five professional website templates that you can use to build your own website within minutes.

This book includes a CD with five website templates, along with software for editing the web templates. In this chapter, you'll look at the fundamental building blocks of websites, and then step through the installation process of Mozilla Composer, the web page creation software included on the CD. In the next chapter you'll examine the necessary steps to create a website, and see how to move the web page templates from the CD to your website. The remaining five chapters of the book examine each of the five templates, illustrating how these templates can be customized for your site.

Each website template is designed for use on a particular type of website. While there are literally millions of websites available on the Internet, virtually all fall into one of five categories:

- ▶ **Family/Personal Website**—Keep your extended family and friends up to date with the latest happenings of your family.

- ▶ **Hobby Website**—Share pictures, tips, tricks, and information about your hobby to others who are also involved in the same hobby.

- ▶ **Websites for an Organization**—Provide information about local organizations—such as social clubs or churches.

- ▶ **Informational Website for a Business**—Promote your business's products and services. Such websites serve as a very cost-effective form of advertising, especially for small family-run operations.

- ▶ **Online Storefront Website**—Sell products and services online! A great revenue stream for home-based businesses.

As you'll see, creating websites that fall into any of these five categories is a snap with the provided templates. To get started, all you'll need is this book, its CD, and access to a computer with Internet connectivity.

"Creating websites is a snap with the provided templates. To get started, all you'll need is this book, its CD, and access to a computer with Internet connectivity."

In this chapter, we will discuss *web pages*, which are the building blocks of any website. We will talk about the tools available for creating and editing web pages, and look at one in particular—Mozilla Composer. Finally, we will build our first web page together, our first step toward building an entire website.

The Components of a Website

In your experiences with the Internet you've likely visited several different websites. Some of the more popular websites in terms of the number of people that visit the site on a daily basis include Yahoo.com, Amazon.com, eBay.com, MSN.com, and others.

In order to visit a website, the computer being used must have an Internet connection. Virtually all computers in places of business have an Internet connection, while millions of home users connect to the Internet through services provided by companies such as AOL, MSN, Earthlink, Juno, or local Internet service providers.

NOTE

Companies that provide Internet connectivity—such as AOL, MSN, and others—are commonly referred to as *ISPs*, which stands for *Internet service provider*.

Visiting a website from an Internet-connected computer is a cinch. Simply open up a *web browser* and type in the *domain name* of the web site into the web browser's Address bar.

NEW TERM

Each website has a unique *domain name*. To view a particular website, a user simply types in the domain name of the website she wants to visit in her browser's Address bar. We'll discuss the purpose of domain names in more detail shortly.

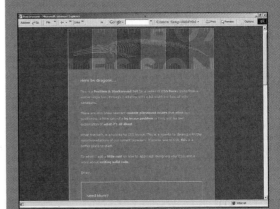

WHO SAYS A GOOD SITE HAS TO BE COLORFUL?

We picked this site for two reasons. First of all, it's a clean, interesting, and simple design that looks great without color. Second, it's a useful site for those of you just learning how to build websites in that it gives you tips and advice on CSS—Cascading Style Sheets.

So many sites are filled with jumbles of color and bright flashing animations that it's hard to know where to click. This site contains only shades of gray with header graphics contained at the top of each page and a simple one-column design. It's very elegant.

This site's designer does a lot of nice things to keep his navigation simple for his users. He adds links within his paragraphs to illustrate his points or send you to other useful sites. This site reads like an instructional book or guide. Unlike some commercial sites that give you a million places to jump from just one page, this designer keeps the messages simple and allows you to stay focused on one topic at a time.

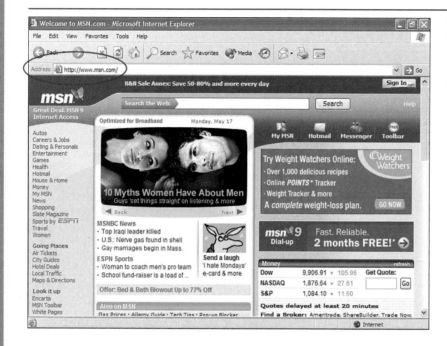

FIGURE 1.1
The MSN website is
displayed in the web
browser.

Figure 1.1 shows a screenshot of the MSN website when viewed through Internet Explorer.

Notice that Figure 1.1 has the browser's Address bar circled. To visit MSN's website simply enter the domain name of the site—www.msn.com—into the browser's Address bar. That's all you have to do.

Before you begin creating your own web pages, it is vital that you know the basic components inherent to all websites. Specifically, all websites are made up of the following three components:

▶ **A Web Server**—A web server is an Internet-connected computer whose sole purpose is to provide a location for the web pages of a website and to handle incoming requests for these web pages.

▶ **A Domain Name**—A website's domain name is a unique identifier for a website, much like your mailing address is a unique identifier for your home. A website's domain name identifies the web server on which the site's web pages are located.

▶ **Web Pages**—A collection of files that make up the content of a website.

Serving Web Pages with a Web Server

All websites are located on a special type of computer referred to as a *web server*, which is an Internet-accessible computer that holds the contents of a specific website.

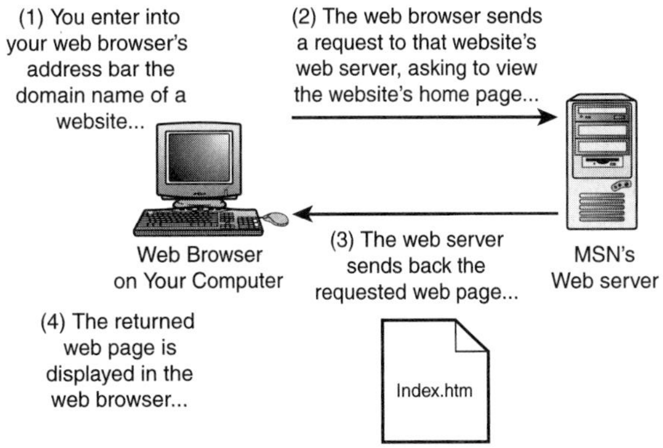

FIGURE 1.2

Visiting a web page involves a request to a web server.

(1) You enter into your web browser's address bar the domain name of a website...

(2) The web browser sends a request to that website's web server, asking to view the website's home page...

Web Browser on Your Computer

(3) The web server sends back the requested web page...

MSN's Web server

(4) The returned web page is displayed in the web browser...

Index.htm

When visiting a website through a web browser, the web browser makes a *request* to the web server that hosts that particular website. The web server then returns the requested web page to the browser. Finally, the browser displays the web page, as was shown in Figure 1.1.

Figure 1.2 details this interaction from a high-level view.

If the details of this interaction seem a bit hazy, don't worry; you don't need to be concerned about the specifics. For now, just realize that the contents of a website reside on a remote computer that, like your computer, is connected to the Internet. The browser obtains the contents of the website you are visiting by making a request to the site's web server. The web server returns the web pages being requested, which are then displayed in the browser.

Understanding Website Domain Names

Did you know that there are literally *millions* of websites in existence? In order to visit a particular website from the list of millions, it is vital that all websites can be uniquely identified in some manner. The way websites are uniquely identified is by their *domain name*.

A domain name is, ideally, an easily remembered phrase, like eBay.com, Yahoo.com, or CNN.com. All domain names end with some sort of *extension*, which is a period followed by two or more letters. Most domain names end with extensions like .com, .net, or .org. Other extensions are available, though.

NOTE

Domain names provide a means to uniquely identify a website.

Web Pages, the Building Blocks of a Website

Web pages are the atomic pieces of a website; each website is a collection of web pages. When visiting a website with a web browser, what you are actually viewing is an individual web page.

On a website, each web page is, in actuality, a separate *file*. A file is a document that's stored on a computer. For example, if you use Microsoft Word to write a letter to your nephew, you can save the letter. This saved letter is referred to as a file.

Each web page is uniquely identified by a *URL*. A *URL*, or *Uniform Resource Locator*, uniquely identifies each and every web page on a website. A URL typically looks like http://domainName/WebPageFileName. For example, if a website's domain name is www.myDomain.com, the web page with the filename Pictures.html would have the URL http://www.myDomain.com/Pictures.html. Each web page on the Internet is addressed by a URL.

You can request a particular web page from a website by typing the web page's URL into a web browser. You don't have to type in a URL to view a web page. As we saw earlier in Figure 1.1, typing in *just* the domain name of a website displays a web page as well. When typing in just the domain name of a website, a specific web page is automatically loaded—this page is referred to as the *home page*.

Getting Around a Website

A website is composed of a number of web pages. Each web page is uniquely identified by a URL. To visit a particular web page, you can enter the web page's URL in your browser's Address bar. However, as you know from surfing the Web on your own, rarely, if ever, do you take the time to enter a URL directly into the browser's Address bar.

An easier way to visit a particular web page is by first loading a website's home page, and then clicking on *hyperlinks* that take you to other pages on the site. Hyperlinks are clickable regions on a web page that, when clicked, whisk you to some other, specified web page. Hyperlinks are the means by which the web pages of a website are navigated.

> **TIP**
>
> Think of a website as a book, and a web page as a page in a book. When visiting a website you can navigate through the various web pages, just like when picking up a book you can flip around to different pages. You navigate through the pages of a book by thumbing through the pages; for a website, you navigate through its web pages by clicking on hyperlinks.

To demonstrate page navigation in a website, take a moment to visit the NBA's website at www.nba.com. As Figure 1.3 shows, this website (like all websites), has a number of hyperlinks. For example, you can click on the Players hyperlink for more information on the game's players, or the Standings hyperlink for a look at the current standings.

FIGURE 1.3

Visiting a web page involves a request to a web server.

Clicking on the Players hyperlink whisks you to a new URL— **http://www.nba.com/statistics/**—which is shown in Figure 1.4. Notice that the Address bar in Figure 1.3 differs from that in Figure 1.4. In Figure 1.3, the Address bar reads http://www.nba.com, the domain name of the NBA website. After clicking on the Statistics hyperlink, we are taken to a different URL. The Address bar has been updated accordingly, illustrating that we are viewing a different web page.

NOTE

If you visit NBA.com while reading this book, the screenshots in Figures 1.3 and 1.4 may appear slightly different. That's because, unlike a book, a website is dynamic, allowing for its contents to be changed easily.

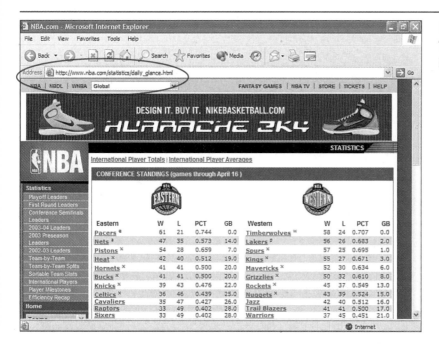

FIGURE 1.4
The Statistics web page is displayed.

Figure 1.5 shows the interactions that take place between the web browser and the NBA.com web server when first visiting the NBA.com home page, and then when clicking on the Daily Glance hyperlink. (Again, if you do not fully understand this interaction, don't sweat it!)

Table 1.1 summarizes the core pieces of a website.

TABLE 1.1	Key Website Building Blocks
Building Block	**Description**
Web Server	A web server is an Internet-accessible computer that hosts one or more websites. When viewing a web page, your browser sends a request to the web server for the specified URL.
Website	A website is a collection of related Web pages. Websites have a bevy of purposes: They can be used to share pictures, provide information, or even sell products. Each website is uniquely identified with a domain name.
Web Page	A web page can have a mix of text and graphics. A web page is like a single page in a book. Web pages can be linked to one another using hyperlinks, allowing the visitor to quickly jump from one web page to another.

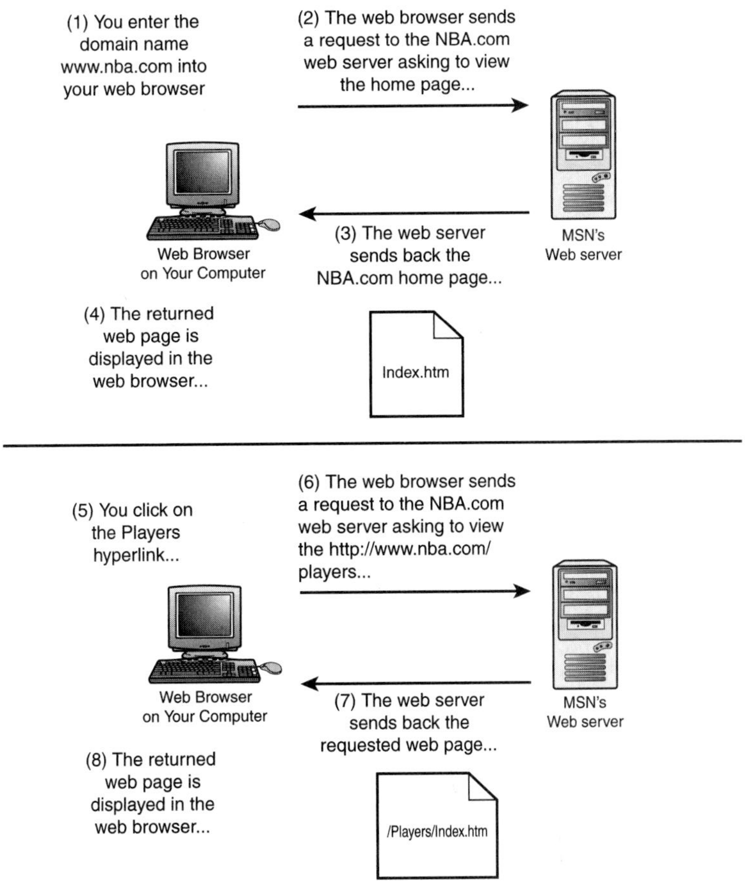

FIGURE 1.5

Each time a new web page is navigated to, the web browser requests the web page from the web server.

(1) You enter the domain name www.nba.com into your web browser

(2) The web browser sends a request to the NBA.com web server asking to view the home page...

Web Browser on Your Computer

MSN's Web server

(3) The web server sends back the NBA.com home page...

(4) The returned web page is displayed in the web browser...

Index.htm

(5) You click on the Players hyperlink...

(6) The web browser sends a request to the NBA.com web server asking to view the http://www.nba.com/ players...

Web Browser on Your Computer

MSN's Web server

(7) The web server sends back the requested web page...

(8) The returned web page is displayed in the web browser...

/Players/Index.htm

Building Web Pages Using Web Page Authoring Software Tools

Creating web pages is a simple task thanks to specially designed web page authoring software tools. These software tools allow you to visually construct a web page with a few points and clicks of the mouse. There are a number of different software packages out there that are designed to make creating web pages a snap. Table 1.2 lists some of the more popular ones, along with their price and a URL to learn more about the product.

GREAT PERSONAL WEBSITE

It seems like everyone has a blog these days. Most of the searching we did for personal sites were actually weblogs created on sites such as Blogger.com, Tripod.com, BlogStudio.com, or a number of other hosting sites. Others, like this, were created with Movable Type. Blogs look like other web pages except that they work more like an online diary or journal. You can make entries as often as you like and visitors can leave comments if you allow them. We also chose this site because it has great information and links for you as beginning web developers. He recommends some good web design books and sends you to other sites that he thinks are cool or informative.

If you want to find out more about Movable Type, visit their website at http://www.movabletype.org/. They offer some great templates to use if you don't feel like designing your own columns and layout. You can also copy code for common things like RSS feeds, indexing features, comments listings.

TABLE 1.2	Popular Web Page Authoring Tools	
Name	Cost	For More Information…
Microsoft FrontPage	$199.00	http://www.microsoft.com/ frontpage/
Macromedia DreamWeaver	$399.00	http://www.macromedia.com/ software/dreamweaver/
Mozilla Composer	Free!	http://www.mozilla.org/

As you can tell by their prices, Microsoft FrontPage and Macromedia DreamWeaver are targeted toward the professional web developer. They are both world-class products that make building professional-looking websites an absolute breeze. Unfortunately, the price point for both of those products is a bit high for first-time web developers (like yourself).

Fortunately, there is a good, *free* web page authoring tool released by the Mozilla group, called Mozilla Composer.

NOTE

Mozilla is a not-for-profit organization established in 1998. The organization created and maintains a free web browser called Mozilla. The Mozilla web browser includes not just a web browser, but many other tools, including Composer, the web page authoring tool.

The CD accompanying this book contains the Mozilla browser and associated tools. In order to use Mozilla Composer to create web pages, you will need to install the Mozilla browser on your computer. Once you have installed the Mozilla web browser you will be able to start using Mozilla Composer.

NOTE

The CD includes the most recent version of the Mozilla browser at the time of this book's writing, version 1.6. You may optionally download and install the most recent version of Mozilla from the Mozilla website—http://www.mozilla.org. If you do, though, realize that there may be some slight discrepancies between what you will see on your screen and the screenshots in this book.

Installing the Mozilla Browser

The CD accompanying this book includes the Mozilla web browser and Composer software, which you'll need to install on your computer to begin creating your first web page. To begin the installation, insert the CD into your computer. Next, go to My Computer and double-click on the CD-ROM drive. This will list the folders on the CD:

▶ Mozilla
▶ Templates

Open the Mozilla folder. Here you will find the file mozilla-win32-1.6.installer.exe. Double-click this file to begin the installation process. The installation process begins by displaying the Mozilla Setup—Welcome dialog box (shown in Figure 1.6).

Click the Next button to begin the installation. The second screen is the Software License Agreement screen, which provides the license for use of Mozilla and its associated products. Once you have read and agreed to this license, click the Accept button. Doing so will take you to the third screen, the Setup Type dialog box (shown in Figure 1.7). The Setup Type screen

lets you determine what type of setup should be performed. Leave the default choice—Complete—selected, and click Next to continue.

FIGURE 1.6

The Mozilla installation welcome message.

FIGURE 1.7

Choose to do a Complete installation.

The next screen asks if you want to use Mozilla's Quick Launch option. Quick Launch adds an icon to the Windows taskbar, keeping

Mozilla running even when you close it. This provides quicker startup times when you launch Mozilla. This option is unchecked by default, and I would encourage you to leave it unchecked unless you foresee yourself using the Mozilla browser regularly in place of Internet Explorer.

Once you have decided on the Quick Launch option, click Next to proceed to the final installation screen (shown in Figure 1.8). This final screen provides a summary of the components that will be installed.

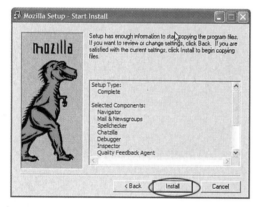

FIGURE 1.8

The final screen reviews the installation options.

Once you are ready to begin the actual installation, click the Install button. Over the next several minutes, Mozilla will be installed on your computer. Once it has completed installation, the Mozilla browser will automatically launch. With Mozilla installed, we are now ready to start using Composer, the web page editing software we'll be using throughout this book.

Starting Mozilla Composer

Once you have installed the Mozilla browser, you are ready to start using Mozilla Composer. To use Composer, you must first launch the Mozilla browser, if it is not running already. To launch Mozilla browser go to the Start menu, choose Programs, go to Mozilla, and select Mozilla.

Once the Mozilla browser has started, you can launch Composer by going to the Window menu in the browser and clicking on the Composer menu item. Alternatively, you can hit Ctrl and the 4 key on your keyboard simultaneously. Figure 1.9 shows a screenshot of the Mozilla browser and the Window menu.

Once you have selected to launch Composer, the Composer window should appear. Figure 1.10 shows a screenshot of the Composer window.

In the next section, we'll examine how to use Composer to create a web page.

TIP

By installing Mozilla Composer, you are also installing a full-fledged web browser as well. The Mozilla web browser has many features not found in Internet Explorer. I would encourage you to try out the Mozilla browser—you might just like it better than Internet Explorer! To learn more about Mozilla's features check out http://mozilla.org/products/mozilla1.x/.

FIGURE 1.9

Launch Composer by selecting Composer from the Window menu.

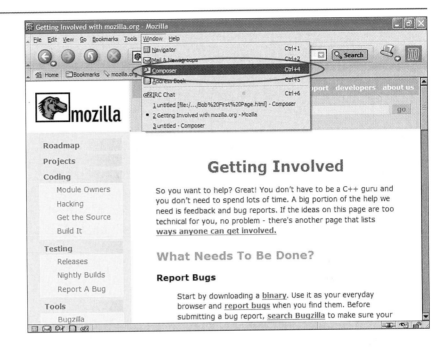

FIGURE 1.10

The Mozilla Composer window.

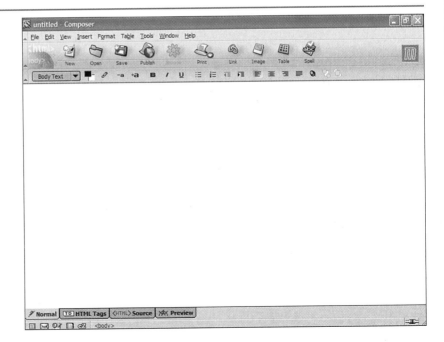

Creating a Web Page with Mozilla Composer

Creating web pages with Mozilla Composer is as easy and intuitive as writing a letter using a program such as Microsoft Word. Let's look at using Composer to build a simple web page, one that provides information about some fictitious individual. We'll start by just entering the content that we want to present in the web page, and will later come back and make the content appear more eye-pleasing.

> *"Creating web pages with Mozilla Composer is as easy and intuitive as writing a letter using a program such as Microsoft Word."*

To follow along, simply start Composer, if you haven't already. Recall that this can be accomplished by launching the Mozilla browser, going to the Window menu, and choosing the Composer option. (Refer back to Figure 1.9 for a screenshot of the Window menu in the Mozilla browser.)

Entering content into the web page is as simple as typing it in! The web page we'll be creating is about a fictitious fellow named Bob. In this page, Bob wants to share information about himself, including

- His age
- What he does for a living
- A bit about his wife and kids
- His hobbies
- Information about his pets

Start out by just typing in the information Bob wants to share with the world. Feel free to be creative and make up a bevy of interesting facts about Bob to share in this web page. I decided to enter the following for Bob:

Hello, you have reached my very first web page! My name is Bob, I'm 34 years old, and I live in Dallas, Texas.

I work as an instructor at a sky-diving school, teaching people how to jump out of planes. I've made over 400 jumps myself, and made my first jump back when I was a mere 12 years old!

I am married to my wife Irene, and we have seven lovely children: Bertha, Bobby-Joe, Jermain, Ted, Todd, Rod, and Lil' Elaine. Bertha's the biggest and oldest, and Lil' Elaine is the youngest (although not the smallest - Rod has that distinction).

For fun I like to bowl. I am in a league, and we play every Wednesday at the Bowlorama.

The joy of my life is my pet parrot, Mr. Polly. Mr. Polly has a large vocabulary, and is quite talkative, especially when the whole family sits down for dinner. Mr. Polly, believe it or not, has been on several jumps with me.

Figure 1.11 shows Composer after I have entered information about Bob.

Without a doubt, Bob's first web page is a bit of a disappointment. It doesn't look very exciting. Over the next several sections we'll examine how Composer allows you to spruce up the appearance of a web page. With a few simple steps you can radically improve the look and feel of a web page.

TIP

If you make a mistake when working with Composer—be it choosing an incorrect color, an incorrect font, mistyping, or whatever—you can undo your last action by going to the Edit menu and selecting Undo.

FIGURE 1.11
Bob's first web page.

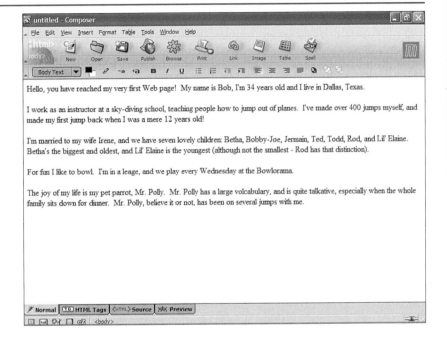

Changing the Font

By default, the text you type into Composer will be displayed using the web browser's default font. You can specify a specific font quite easily in Composer, though. To demonstrate this, let's have Bob's home page displayed in the Arial font.

To accomplish this, start by highlighting all of the text you've typed in thus far. To highlight the text you can go to the Edit menu and choose Select All, or, using the mouse, you can click and hold the button within the text and drag the mouse cursor to select a portion of the text. To change the selected text's font, go to the Format menu and choose the Font option. This will display a long list of available fonts, as shown in Figure 1.12. To follow along, choose the Arial font.

Figure 1.13 shows Composer after the font has been changed to Arial.

NOTE

Most professional web pages are displayed in one of three fonts: Arial, Times New Roman, or Verdana. Figure 1.14 shows the same sentence in these three different fonts.

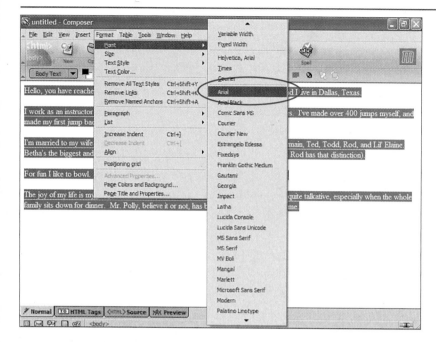

FIGURE 1.12

The Format menu's Font option lists the available fonts.

FIGURE 1.13

The text in Bob's web page is displayed in the Arial font.

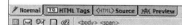

This is an example of Arial.

This is an example of Times New Roman

This is an example of Verdana

FIGURE 1.14

Arial, Times New Roman, and Verdana are the three most popular fonts.

TIP

To change the text for a portion of the document, use the mouse to select just the text whose font you want to change. Then go to the Format menu's Font option and select the font you want to change the selected text to.

Making Text Bold, Italic, and Underlined

You can make text bold, italic, and underlined using the toolbar icons shown circled in Figure 1.15. To apply such formatting to a given piece of text, highlight the text and then click the appropriate icons.

For example, let's have Bob's children's names italicized. To accomplish this, use the mouse to select Bob's children's names. Once this text is selected, simply click the Italic icon (the *I* in the toolbar), and the text will become italicized.

Also, let's add a brief title before each paragraph, where each title is made bold. Figure 1.16 shows Composer after the boldfaced paragraph titles have been added and the children's names italicized.

A GOOD PICTURE IS WORTH A THOUSAND WORDS

This site's pictures are great. Not only do they sell very tiny objects (gemstones), but their pictures are large enough and clear enough to view even the smallest details and cuts of each stone. If you want to sell products through your website or through a site like eBay, get a good digital camera and practice uploading photos to make sure they're attractive, but still small enough to load quickly for the viewer. If your page doesn't load within 30 seconds, visitors will probably leave.

JPEG is a good format for the Web because it compresses images so that they can load faster. Some photo programs such as Adobe's Photoshop Elements have the capabilities to help you save pictures for the Web. They give you choices in a dialog box and they handle the rest—the right compression, image sizing, and color features to make your pictures look great on your site. If you're going to edit photos yourself, here are a few guidelines. Most product pictures on websites are no larger than 400 x 400 pixels. Thaigems's largest pictures are about 200 x 200. The size of the file is important, too. Aim for 50KB or smaller.

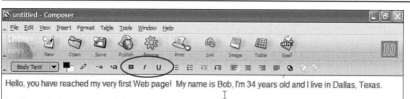

FIGURE 1.15

These toolbar icons allow you to make text bold, italic, and underlined.

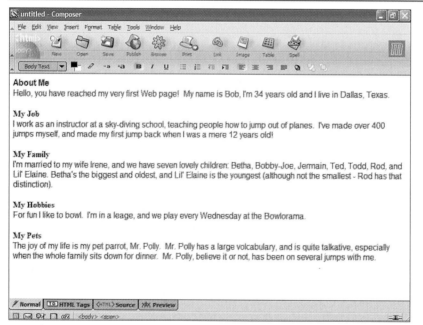

FIGURE 1.16

Some bold and italic formatting has been applied.

Changing the Colors

Composer allows you to easily specify the foreground color for text, and the background color for a web page. To set the foreground color, simply select the text whose color you want to change, and then go to the Format menu and choose the Text Color menu option.

Choosing this option will display the Text Color dialog box, which is shown in Figure 1.17.

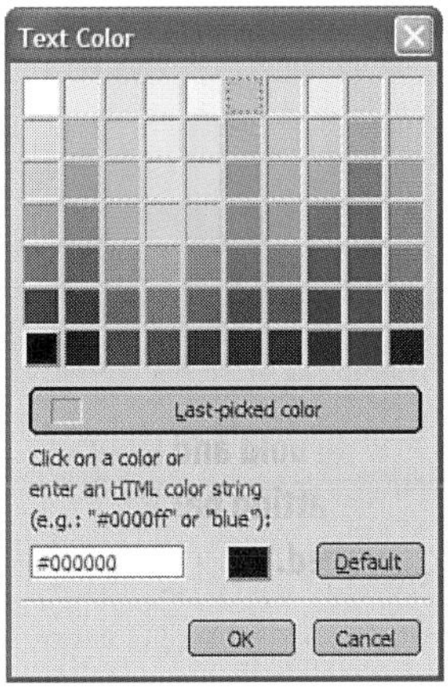

FIGURE 1.17

The Text Color dialog box allows you to select the text's color.

This dialog box allows you to choose a color from a palette of colors. Upon selecting a color and clicking the OK button, the dialog box will close and the selected text's foreground color will change to the specified color. Take a moment to alter the foreground color of some text in Bob's web page.

The web page's background color can be changed by going to the Format menu and choosing the Page Colors and Backgrounds option. This will display the Page Colors and Backgrounds dialog box (shown in Figure 1.18). To change the page's background color, select the Use custom colors radio button and then click on the Background button. This will display the Text Color dialog box shown in Figure 1.17. After choosing a color and clicking

OK in both dialog boxes, you will be returned to Composer and the background color will have changed to the specified color.

FIGURE 1.18

This dialog box allows you to change the background color of the web page.

TIP

When specifying colors, be sure that the background and foreground colors contrast so that the text is readable. If you choose a dark text color on a dark background, or a light text color on a light background, visitors to your web page won't be able to read the text!

Some examples of bad color choices include yellow text on a white background and blue text on a black background.

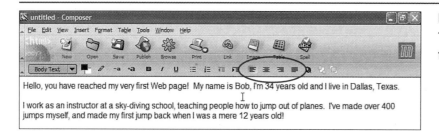

FIGURE 1.19

These toolbar icons allow for positioning of text.

Positioning Text

Like with a word processor, Composer allows you to position text in one of four ways:

- Left-aligned
- Center-aligned
- Right-aligned
- Justified

To specify the positioning, simply select the text you wish to position and then choose the appropriate positioning icon from the toolbar. Figure 1.19 shows the text-alignment toolbar icons circled.

To practice text positioning, take a moment to right-align all of the paragraph titles (About Me, My Job, and so on). To right-align the About Me title, simply select the text and then click the right-align toolbar icon. Repeat this process for all paragraph titles on the page.

Figure 1.20 shows Composer after the right-aligning has been performed.

Saving the Web Page

There are many more formatting options in Composer, and we will examine these in detail when we start building full-blown websites. The goal of the past few sections was to introduce you to some of the more basic formatting options Composer provides, and to hammer home the concept that formatting in Composer is synonymous to formatting text in a word processor.

"There are many more formatting options in Composer, and we will examine these in detail when we start building full-blown websites."

Now that you have completed Bob's first web page, save it. To save the web page, go to the File menu and choose the Save option. This will display a dialog box prompting us for the *title* for this web page.

NEW TERM
All web pages have a *title* associated with them. The title is what is displayed in the web browser's title bar when the page is visited.

FIGURE 1.20

The paragraph titles are now right-aligned.

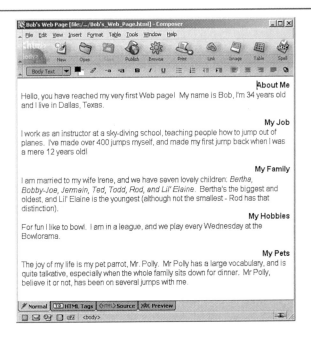

Choose a title, such as "Bob's First Web Page" and click OK. Next, you will be prompted for where to save the file. You can save it anywhere on your computer you'd like, such as in the My Documents folder, on the Desktop, or in a custom folder. You can open this web page for further editing at a future time by starting Composer, going to the File menu, and then choosing the Open option.

At this point, the web page is saved only on your computer. There is no way that your grandmother in Toledo could visit this web page through her web browser. In order to make this web page accessible to anyone with an Internet connection, we will need to create a website and then copy this file to the web server that hosts our website. This involves a number of steps, which we'll examine in detail in the next chapter.

Summary

With the completion of this chapter you've taken your first step in your journey to create websites. This chapter was a big first step, covering many important facets of websites, web pages, and web page authoring tools.

This chapter began by looking at the three things all websites have:

▶ A web server to return the requested web pages to the requesting web browsers

▶ A domain name, to uniquely identify the website

▶ Web pages, which make up the building blocks of a website

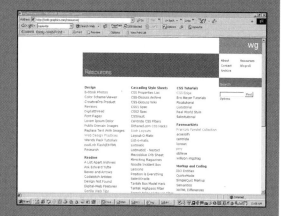

WEB RESOURCES GALORE

We thought this was a great resource site for those of you getting into web design and development. The links are divided into categories such as CSS (cascading style sheet) tutorials, design and web graphics, markup resources, and places to find stock photos and illustrations. This is a page that you can bookmark and visit whenever you need something for your site or when you're ready to learn some new trick. In the miscellaneous section, there's even a link to some nice little demos on Javascript flexible floats, image captions, titles, and CSS drop shadows.

What if you want to know how other people are setting up their web pages for the best user experience? Click on the link for web design practices, and you'll find help with navigation, e-commerce functions, and page layout. There are people whose only job is to analyze the usability of websites. Why not take advantage of this free advice?

A web server is a computer where a website's web pages reside. It is this web server that is queried when a user visits the website through a web browser. The domain name is a unique identifier for a website. To visit the home page for a particular website, simply enter the domain name in your web browser's Address bar. Finally, a website is composed of one to many web pages. Each web page is, in actuality, a file residing on the web server. Web pages contain HTML markup that specifies how their content should be displayed in a web browser.

In this chapter, you also saw how to use Mozilla Composer to create a simple web page. Composer enables you to create and edit web pages just like you would work with documents in any word processor program. Before you can start using Composer, though, you first need to install the Mozilla software located on this book's accompanying CD.

In the next chapter, "Creating a Website," we'll take a deeper look at the communication interactions involved between a web browser and a web server. We'll also look at how to get started creating a website, which involves finding a web host provider and registering a domain name. Finally, we'll see how to upload web pages from your computer onto your public website's web server. All this and more in the next chapter!

CHAPTER 2

Creating a Website

In the previous chapter, you examined how to use Composer to create your first web page. After creating the web page, you saved the web page to a folder on your computer. While storing the web page on your computer allows you to easily update the web page at some time in the future, it does not permit others to view your web page via a web browser. That is, when the web page is stored just on your computer, you are the only person who can view your web page.

In order to share a web page with the world, you need to create a *website*.

A *website* is a set of documents on a computer with a permanent connection to the Internet, whose web pages are accessible to anyone with an Internet connection. Creating a website involves three steps:

1. Contact a *web host provider* and obtain a public website.

2. Register a *domain name*, such as www.MyFirstWebSite.com, and have the domain name registered with the website.

3. Upload your web pages to the public website.

Once you accomplish these three steps, your web pages will be able to be viewed by anyone connected to the Internet! As discussed in the previous chapter, people will be able to visit your website by simply opening a web browser and typing in your website's domain name into the Address bar.

"In order to share a web page with the world, you need to create a website."

In this chapter, you will learn how to accomplish each of these three steps. If you follow along, by the end of this chapter you will have a publicly available website that you can share with your friends, family, and customers!

Finding a Web Host Provider

The first step in creating a public website is finding a *web host provider*. A web host provider is a company that offers a computer that is connected to the Internet 24 hours a day, seven days a week. This computer functions as a web server—that is, it does nothing but wait for incoming requests from remote web browsers. Upon receiving a request, it returns the requested web page.

There are multitudes of web host providers, from small one-man companies to Fortune 100 companies publicly traded on the stock market. Costs, too, run the gamut, all the way from free to several thousand dollars per month.

Given the sheer number of web host providers, finding a web host provider is not challenging in the least. Simply go to any search engine and type in "web hosting company" into the search box. Such a search at Google.com provides an estimated 6.7 million matching results!

Another approach is to use one of the many websites that serve as a "white pages" of web hosting companies. Sites such as TopHosts (www.tophosts.com), HostIndex (www.hostindex.com), and HostSearch (www.hostsearch.com) provide a searchable index of thousands of web hosting companies around the world.

If you want to save the hassle of searching for a web host provider through a search engine or a host index-type site, consider asking your Internet service provider (ISP) if they offer web hosting.

NOTE

Your ISP is the company that provides your computer with Internet access. Common ISPs are companies such as AOL, Earthlink, MSN, and many phone companies, such as SBC.

TIP

ISPs often make for ideal web host providers because oftentimes a web hosting account is included in the monthly price paid for Internet service. With other web hosting companies, you'll need to pay some monthly fee for the services provided.

Important Web Hosting Metrics

When researching web hosting companies, you'll find that they all toss around various technical sounding facts, like, "We offer 250MB of disk space and a monthly transfer limit of 2GB!" To help make sense of this technical and marketing mumbo-jumbo, let's take a moment to examine some of the common technical benchmarks used.

Disk Space

Oftentimes web hosting companies limit you to storing only a certain amount of data on the web server. This number can range from web host to web host, but typically a web host will allow you to store several megabytes (MB) on the web server.

The amount of web space you'll need depends on what you plan on storing on your website. If you plan on just having web pages and some pictures, 20MB should be more than enough. Realize that each picture taken from a digital camera can consume anywhere from 50 kilobytes (KB) to 250KB, depending on the quality and settings of the camera. (A megabyte is approximately 1,000 kilobytes.)

So, assuming your digital camera takes pictures that are 250KB, the upper bound, you could store four pictures per megabyte. If you wanted to share, say, 25 pictures, then you'd need 6,250KB, or 6.25MB. As you can see, a 20MB account is usually sufficient for most peoples' websites, but if you anticipate posting large amounts of pictures, or other files that are exceptionally large in size, you will want to choose a web host that provides your anticipated disk space needs.

Monthly Transfer Limit

Every time someone visits a web page from a website, the website must transfer the contents of the web pages, and any pictures on the web page, to the requesting web browser. The more data transferred from a web server, the more cost is incurred by the web host provider. Therefore, to keep costs down, many web host providers specify some sort of monthly transfer cap for a website.

"For small personal sites, a 2GB transfer limit is typically more than enough."

A FEW WORDS ABOUT CSS—CASCADING STYLE SHEETS

If you're going to be a professional web developer, you'll eventually want to move away from tables and start implementing CSS. Adactio was the best place we found to help you make this leap. There are many resources out on the Web to help you. Mezzoblue is great, too (http://www.mezzoblue.com/css/cribsheet/). We chose Adactio, though, because this site's designer took the time to create a really great introduction into the discipline of CSS. He takes you through the Web that you already know and into the future of web design with style sheets. He explains why it's a good thing to separate your content from your layout and structure. In the end, you'll find that CSS may take some planning and a little more setup time, but the results are worth the effort. In a nutshell, here's what he says:

"Just imagine all the benefits that come with separating your presentation from your content.

"Your pages will be smaller, much smaller. Without the bloat that comes with nested tables, spacer images and font tags, your markup will be leaner and meaner. That will appeal to search engines.

> **NOTE**
> The monthly transfer limit is sometimes referred to as the *monthly bandwidth*.

Typical monthly transfer limits are in the range of 2 gigabytes (GB) to 10GB. (One gigabyte is approximately 1,000 megabytes.) Some web hosts use the monthly transfer limit as a *hard limit*. That is, if the monthly bandwidth exceeds the limit, the website is shut down for the remainder of the month. Other web hosts use the limit as a *soft limit*, meaning that after the monthly limit is exceeded, a specified cost per exceeded GB is tacked on to the monthly web hosting service fees. And other websites don't impose a monthly transfer limit at all.

For small personal sites, a 2GB transfer limit is typically more than enough. To put things in perspective, consider that your website has content totaling 10MB of disk space. Assume that each visitor ends up viewing on average 2MB worth of pictures and other content. Now, assume that you have 250 visitors per month, that knocks the monthly bandwidth up to 500MB, or 0.5GB.

Of course, if you expect a deluge of visitors, 2GB might not be enough. If you think your site will be heavily trafficked, or you plan on hosting content that is large in file size (such as home videos, MP3s of songs you've written, or other large files), you might want to choose a web hosting company that does not impose a monthly bandwidth limit.

FTP Support

At some point, you will need to move the web pages you've created with Composer from your local machine to the web host company's web server. A very common means for transferring files from one computer to another over the Internet is *FTP*. FTP stands for *File Transfer Protocol*, and is the de facto protocol for transferring files between remote computers. Composer uses the FTP protocol to upload files from your local computer to the host's web server. Therefore, it is vital that the web hosting company you choose to go with supports FTP access. See Table 2.1 for some important web host terms.

> *"...A number of free web hosting companies, such as GeoCities (www.geocities.com), offer a free website, but require that you pay a nominal monthly fee for FTP access."*

Virtually all web host companies provide FTP access. The thing to watch out for, though, is that a number of free web hosting companies, such as GeoCities (**www.geocities.com**), offer a free website, but require that you pay a nominal monthly fee for FTP access. Therefore, make sure that the plan you choose to go with does include FTP support so that you can transfer your web pages from Composer to the web server.

TABLE 2.1	Important Web Host Terms
Metric	**Description**
Disk Space	Web hosts typically limit the amount of web pages, images, and other files that you can have on your website. If you plan on storing many large images on your site, be sure to choose a web hosting plan with adequate disk space.
Monthly Transfer Limit	To help manage data transfer costs, web hosting companies typically place a limit on your site's bandwidth. For small web sites, 2 gigabytes of monthly bandwidth are typically more than sufficient. However, if you're planning on building a widely trafficked site, make sure you choose a web hosting plan with sufficient transfer limits.
FTP Access	In order to upload your web pages from Composer to your web server, the web hosting company will need to provide FTP access.

Picking a Web Hosting Company

Once you have researched a variety of web hosting companies, it is time to pick one of them and sign up! Web host companies typically charge an initial setup fee along with a recurring monthly fee.

Most large ISPs provide web hosting support along with the paid Internet connectivity, so you might first want to check with your ISP and see what they can offer web hosting-wise.

Before you sign up with a web hosting company I would strongly encourage you to first check—and then double-check—that the company provides FTP support for the plan you are signing up for. Remember, FTP support is needed so that Composer can be used to upload the web pages.

Registering a Domain Name

Recall from Chapter 1, "Creating Your First Web Page," that to visit a website, you just need to type the website's domain name into the browser's Address bar. If you want a domain name for your website, such as www.MyFirstWebSite.com, you'll need to register the domain name you want and configure the domain name to point to the web hosting company's web server.

> **NOTE**
>
> Realize that you do not need to associate a domain name with your website. If you do not, though, your website's address will be something like: http://www.WebHostCompanyName.com/YourWebSiteName. With a domain name, however, your website will be accessible by something more personalized, like http://www.YourWebSiteName.com.

To register a domain name, we need to perform the following two steps:

1. Choose and then purchase an available domain name.

2. Configure the domain name so that it references the correct website.

Over the next two sections we'll look at how to accomplish these two steps. Don't worry if these sound like daunting tasks; as we'll see

shortly, they both are relatively simple to perform, even for the computer layperson.

> **TIP**
>
> If you are concerned about performing these two steps on your own, understand that most web hosting companies will perform these steps for you for free or for a nominal charge. If you'd rather leave this to a professional, simply ask your web host if they can register a domain name for you.

Choosing and Buying a Domain Name

When registering a domain name, you can only choose a domain name that has not been registered by someone else. That is, you cannot take an existing domain name—say www.microsoft.com—and register that domain name, having it point to your website. So, the first step in registering a domain name is finding and selecting an available domain name.

Domain names can be purchased from a variety of domain name registrars. A *domain name registrar* is a company that is sanctioned by the Internet Corporation for Assigned Names and Numbers (ICANN) to allow registration of domain names. There are dozens of such companies available, varying in price and quality of service. A complete list can be found at http://www.icann.org/registrars/accredited-list.html.

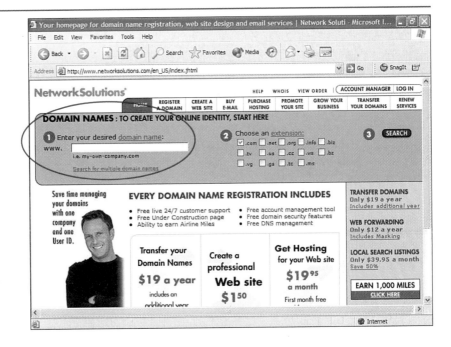

FIGURE 2.1
The Network Solutions home page lets you search for available domain names.

NOTE

When purchasing a domain name, you are not buying the domain name outright. Rather, you are essentially leasing the domain name for a specified period of time (between one and ten years). After this period of time has ended, as the registrant of the domain name you can re-register the domain name for another period of time, or you can release the domain name, returning it to the pool of available domain names.

A common registrar used is Network Solutions (www.networksolutions.com). At the time of this writing, they charge $35.00 to register the domain name for one year, or less per year if registering for multiple years. Before a domain name can be registered, though, it must be available.

To determine if a domain name is available, start by going to any domain name registrar company's website, such as www.networksolutions.com. These companies will typically have a search box on their site to search for available domain names. Figure 2.1 shows the Network Solutions home page. Notice that there is a text box that lets you enter a domain name, along with what extensions you want to search on (.com, .org, .net, .info, and so forth).

Upon searching for a domain name, you will see whether or not the domain names are available. If they are, you can register for them, choosing how long to register the domain name. If the name is already taken, a list of similar domain names is suggested. Figure 2.2 shows the results of a search for the domain name ScottsFirstWebSite searching on extensions .com, .org, and .net.

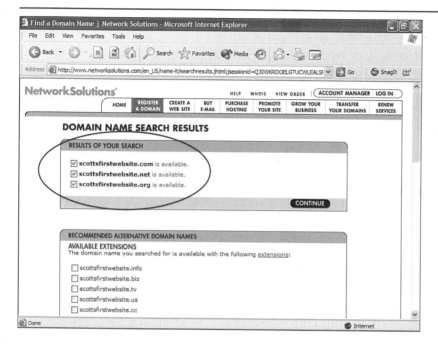

FIGURE 2.2

Searching on a domain name returns a list of available domain names, along with similar domain names and extensions.

To register the checked domain names, simply click the Continue button. This will take you through a checkout process, where you specify the duration of the domain name registration, and provide your credit card number for payment.

Configuring the Domain Name

Sometime during the domain name registration process, you will be asked to provide the *IP address* for the *name servers* you want the domain name to point to. While these terms may sound like Greek to you, the web hosting company is familiar with these terms, and can help you out. Simply ask the web hosting company what name server IP addresses to use—they'll provide you with, typically, two IP addresses that you can enter as the primary

and secondary name server addresses. (An IP address is a number of the form XXX.XXX.XXX.XXX, where XXX is a number between 0 and 255.)

NOTE

Realize that there can be a 24- to 72-hour delay after registering and configuring a domain name and before the domain name officially points to the appropriate web server. That means that it can take a few days after registering your domain name before anyone can visit your website by directly entering the domain name into their web browser.

At this point, you have chosen a web hosting provider and, perhaps, registered a domain name. The only piece of the puzzle that's left is adding web pages, images, and other files to the web server. This is accomplished by uploading the web pages we create in Composer to the web server.

Uploading Web Pages from Composer to Your Website

In order to upload web pages from Composer to your public website, you will first need to procure some information from your web hosting company. The pertinent information, which was likely emailed to you when you signed up with the web hosting company, is

- ▶ The FTP server to upload your files
- ▶ Your username and password to access the FTP server

Armed with this information, you are ready to upload a web page from Composer to your website.

First, you must have a web page to upload. In the remaining chapters of this book, you'll be examining five different website templates. Each template is composed of a series of web pages. To create a website, you'll take the

THE SECRETS OF COLOR COMBINATIONS

Adam Polselli, the creator of this site, is very talented. We chose this site because he reveals how he chooses color combinations, but it's just a great site in general. Browse around and you'll find all kinds of goodies, including good writing, beautiful photographs, and some links to the tools he uses to create such a wonderful site.

His color scheme page shows you how he takes photos and picks colors from them to create color combinations that work for his Web page. So we tried it ourselves and it worked! Here's how to do it.

1. Open any simple paint program on your computer; it doesn't have to be Adobe Photoshop or anything expensive. We used the paint program that comes with the Microsoft operating system.

2. Open a photo that you find attractive.

3. Use the "pick color" tool that looks like an eye-dropper and click on a particular shade in the photo that you like

4. You'll see that the color you "picked" is available in your paint palette in your toolbox now.

It's that simple. Let nature choose your color scheme.

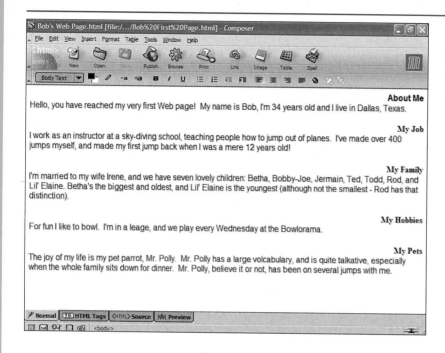

FIGURE 2.3

The first web page we created back in Chapter 1.

templates from the CD, customize them for your site, and then upload the modified templates to your website. Since you've yet to examine these templates, for now upload the practice web page you created (and saved) in Chapter 1. Start by opening the web page we created in Chapter 1 by launching Composer, then going to the File menu and choosing the Open File menu option.

Once you have opened this web page, your screen should look similar to Figure 2.3.

Now, upload this web page to your public web server. To do so, go to the File menu and choose the Publish menu option (see Figure 2.4).

This will display the Publish Page dialog box. The Publish Page dialog box has two tabs: Publish and Settings. When first publishing a page to a public website, you will be taken to the Settings tab (shown in Figure 2.5), where you are prompted for the website's name, its FTP server, the web address, and the FTP server login information (username and password).

In the Publishing address text box, enter the name of the FTP server your web host provider told you to use. In the HTTP address of your home page text box, enter the URL for your website. In the User name and Password text boxes, enter the username and password you were given to access the FTP server. After you have provided this information once, you will not need to enter it again.

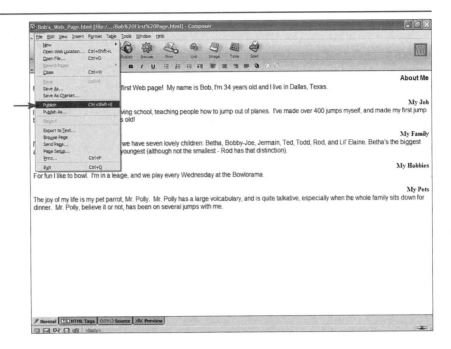

Upon entering this information into the Settings tab, click on the Publish tab. This tab, shown in Figure 2.6, allows you to optionally specify the web page's title, and requires that you specify a filename for the web page. Remember from our discussions in Chapter 1 that web pages are actually stored as files on the web server. Therefore, you need to provide a filename for this web page. For the web pages you'll be creating throughout this book, be sure to name your files with the extension .htm or .html.

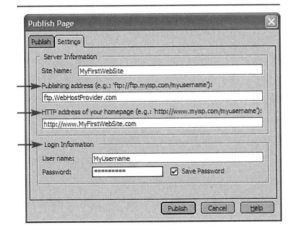

NOTE

Recall from Chapter 1 that the title of a web page appears in the title of the web browser when visiting the page.

JUST GIVE ME A TEMPLATE!

What if you're not creative? What if you have no design education and experience at all? You still want a nice looking website that attracts visitors, and you have the skills to create it, but you need the look—the typefaces, the colors, the art. We just had to review Adam Polselli's site again for this very reason—he offers you an array of choices from simple chic to corporate to vintage and tells you step by step how to get the particular look that you want. After you read through his reasons for choosing elements to achieve his theme, he lets you click on a link called "Putting It All Together," where you'll see a bulleted list of typefaces he recommends, color schemes, shapes, borders, and photo finishes so that you can duplicate his design.

If you still want more than instructions to achieve a look, then you can buy HTML templates from websites. Try sites like Boxedart.com and designload.net, where you can buy full page templates or just buttons, art, and logos.

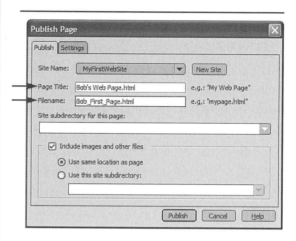

FIGURE 2.6

Set the web page's title and filename in the Publish Page dialog box's Publish tab.

After providing a title and filename click the Publish button. This will display the Publishing dialog box, and report on the status of the web page upload. Figure 2.7 shows the Publishing dialog box after the file has been successfully uploaded.

FIGURE 2.7

Bob's web page has been successfully uploaded.

FIGURE 2.8

Bob's website is now online, accessible by anyone with an Internet connection!

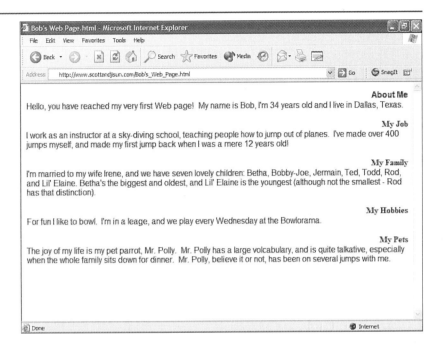

FIGURE 2.8

Bob's website is now online, accessible by anyone with an Internet connection!

NOTE

If you get an error when trying to publish a web page, the error may be due to an incorrect FTP server name, or invalid login credentials. Go to File, Publish As, and re-enter the FTP location and FTP credentials in the Settings tab. If you still experience problems, contact your web hosting provider for further assistance.

Once you have uploaded the web page, you can visit the web page through a web browser. To do so, enter into the browser's Address bar the URL to your website—either the domain name, if you have one, or the URL provided by your web hosting company, such as http://www.webhostingcompany.com/YourWebSite— followed by the name of the web page you

uploaded. So, to visit Bob's web page, which was named Bob's_Web_Page.html, you could visit the page by entering http://www.YourDomainName.com/Bob's_Web_Page.html or http://www.webhostprovider.com/YourWebSite/ Bob's_Web_Page.html. Figure 2.8 shows a screenshot of visiting Bob's web page on my public website, whose domain name is http://www.ScottAndJisun.com.

Building a Website from a Template

The CD accompanying this book contains web pages for five templates. When creating your own websites, you'll want to start with one of these five templates, customizing the template's pages for your site's particular content. In the book's remaining chapters, you'll learn various tips for modifying these templates. For now, it is important to understand the process you'll need to take in order to modify a template on the CD.

"The CD accompanying this book contains web pages for five templates. When creating your own websites, you'll want to start with one of these five templates, customizing the template's pages for your site's particular content."

To start, you'll want to copy the template's files from the CD to your computer's hard drive. From there, you can use Composer to tweak each template file, saving the changes. Also, you may want to include additional pages for your site, using the provided template's look and feel. To summarize the process, when building a site from a template, you'll want to perform the following steps:

1. Create a new folder on your computer's hard drive.

2. Copy all of the template's files from the CD to the folder created in step 1.

3. Launch Composer. Recall that this is accomplished by running Mozilla, and then going to the Window menu and choosing the Composer menu option.

4. Open one of the template files copied to the folder in step 2. You can also add a new web page to your site by creating a page in Composer based on the template.

5. Customize the template file's contents for your website.

6. Save the changes made to the template file.

You'll want to repeat steps 4 through 6 for each of the files in the template. Once you have customized and saved each of the pages in the template, the final step is to publish the website to a web server, so that anyone with an Internet connection can view your site. The publishing process is described at the end of each of the remaining chapters.

Summary

In this chapter, you learned the steps necessary for creating a public website, which include

▶ Finding a web host provider

▶ Registering a domain name (optional)

▶ Uploading web pages from Composer to the web server

As discussed, there are numerous web host providers available that you can chose from, varying in price, service, and features offered. Thankfully there are entire websites—like TopHosts.com and HostIndex.com—that act as search engines for web host providers. Rather than using a separate web hosting company, your Internet service provider (ISP) might also provide web hosting capabilities for free. When selecting a web hosting company, be sure to choose one whose disk space and monthly transfer limits meet your site's needs, and one that provides FTP access.

After choosing a company to host your website, you can optionally register a domain name, giving your website a personalized, memorable name, like www.YourWebSite.com. A domain name can be leased for one to ten years using a domain name registrar, like Network Solutions. When registering a domain name, you'll need to know the IP address of your web host company's name servers. This information associates your domain name with your website. (For more information on this process, refer to the "Understanding How the Internet Works" section in the Bonus Chapter.)

Once you have selected a web host provider, you can upload web pages from your personal computer to your website, so that anyone with an Internet connection can view your pages. If you followed along in acquiring a web hosting provider, registering a domain name, and uploading files, you should now have a publicly accessible website that can be visited by anyone in the world with an Internet connection!

With the information covered in this chapter and the previous one, you have enough knowledge to start creating your own website! The remainder of this book—Chapters 3 through 7—explore five different templates that you can quickly and easily modify to build different types of websites.

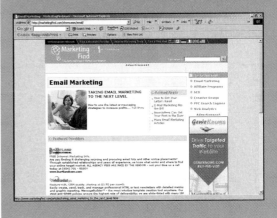

IF YOU BUILD IT, THEY WILL COME (RIGHT?)

Marketing Find was the best site we found that tells you how to let people know about your website. There are so many ways to reach customers through the Internet—email newsletters and promotions, online ads, and paying for words on search engines such as Google. How do you know what's cost effective? How do you measure success? This site is like a mini Internet marketing class. Check out their article and recommended resources for analyzing your website traffic called "Yo! Analyze This!" Want to do email marketing, but don't know how to get your customer's attention? This site has an entire section devoted to email marketing and newsletters. Even the ads on this site are a great resource to you as beginning web developers. We found advertisers who will measure your site traffic for you; others who will create, send, and track your email campaigns; and companies who will drive targeted traffic to your website.

Check out the section of their site called "Marketing Math." They provide an online ROI calculator for you. Just plug some metrics on your advertising campaign and your revenue, and their calculator will tell you if you received a fair return for your investment.

CHAPTER 3

Creating a Family/Personal Website

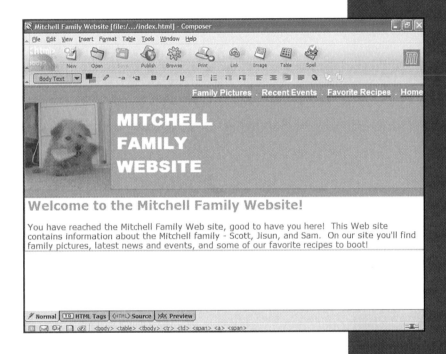

The book's first two chapters looked at the pieces that make up the Internet and websites, and showed how to create simple web pages with Composer. At this point, we're ready to examine how to use Composer to build a complete website. While you can create a website from scratch, it's much easier and quicker to start working with a *website template*. A website template, often referred to as just a *template*, is a collection of generic, pre-made web pages that can be easily customized to create a specific site.

When designing websites, designers typically start with an appropriate template and then tailor the template's pages accordingly. Throughout this book we'll be examining five different templates, starting with a template for a family/personal website.

Examining the Family/Personal Template

Friends and families today are increasingly distant, spread around the country and world. Fortunately, keeping your families and friends up-to-date with what's going on in your life is made remarkably easier with a family/personal website, which provides family and friends a one-stop location to catch up on your life. Most family/personal websites have similar features: pictures of the family or person the website is about, a list of recent happenings, and important upcoming dates, such as anniversaries or birth dates.

As you can see in Figure 3.1, the family/personal website template provided with the book's accompanying CD offers a template that contains the following pages:

- ▶ A home page that gives a brief description of the site and has links to the other web pages.

- ▶ A photo gallery index page, which provides a list of links to various family pictures.

- ▶ A recent news page, which lists the latest family events.

- ▶ A list of recipes for the family's favorite recipes.

In this chapter, you'll examine how you can tailor the family/personal template. As you'll see, it's quite easy to take the provided template and change the look and feel, as well as add and remove content. For example, the pages provided in the template are just a few of many potential web pages that you may want to add to your family/personal website. Other potential pages include

- ▶ The scores from a child's soccer games.

- ▶ Information about children's after-school activities, such as cheerleading or debate.

- ▶ Any other bit of information your extended family or friends might care to hear about!

In the "Customizing the Template" section you'll see just how easy it is to add new pages to your family/personal website.

Before you can start customizing the template, you'll first need to understand how to start working with the template files. Essentially, you'll need to copy the template's files from the CD to your computer's hard drive.

FIGURE 3.1

The family/personal website template.

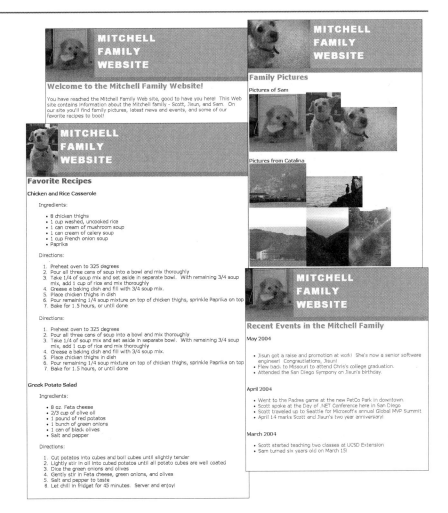

This chapter concludes with a discussion on how to *publish* your website, once you have tailored the template. Publishing a website involves copying the web pages from your computer to the web server computer where your public website is hosted. As we'll see, Composer makes this process a simple one.

Customizing the Template

The family/personal website template shown in Figure 3.1 provides bare-bone web pages that you can easily add to and customize to create your own unique family/personal website. If you like the look and feel of the template, all that's left to do is to customize the template's content, replacing the current text with the text pertinent to you and your family, and the image in the upper-left corner with an image of your own choosing.

"When working with the template, you may find that you want to customize certain aspects... Fortunately, Composer makes customizing the template quick, fun, and easy."

NOTE

Recall that to customize a template you need to copy the template files from the book's accompanying CD to your computer's hard drive. The "Building a Website from a Template" section in Chapter 2, "Creating a Website," provides more details on this process.

When working with the template, you may find that you want to customize certain aspects. For example, you might want to change the template's font, or alter the text or background colors. You might want to add additional web pages to the template, such as a web page that lists important dates (anniversaries, birthdays, and so on). You might want to remove pages from the template; perhaps you don't want a favorite recipes page.

Fortunately, Composer makes customizing the template in any of these ways quick, fun, and easy. In this section, we'll be examining a

myriad of ways to customize your template. When working with the template files, keep the following two things in mind:

▶ Composer is like any other word processor. If you want to customize the page by centering some text, for example, simply select the text to center and click on the Center icon in the toolbar, just like you would to center text with Microsoft Word.

▶ Have fun customizing the templates, and don't be afraid to experiment! Keep in mind that since you're working with the template files on your computer's hard drive, no matter what you do, you can't irreparably screw up the template. There will always be a pristine copy of the website's template files on the book's CD that you can recopy to your computer should the need arise.

With that, it's time to get started examining how to use Composer to customize the family/personal website template!

Changing the Upper-Left Image

Each page in the family/personal website contains an image in the upper-left corner of my dog, Sam. You are invited to add your own image here, such as a picture of yourself, your family, or your family's pet. To replace the picture of Sam with a picture of your own, you'll need to have the picture on your computer's hard drive. In the "Customizing the Family Pictures Page" section, you'll learn how to get pictures of yourself or family onto your computer, so that you can add them to your website's pages.

FIGURE 3.2

The index.html file has been opened with Composer.

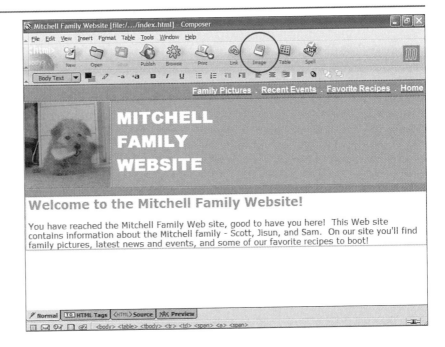

FIGURE 3.2

The index.html file has been opened with Composer.

To customize the upper-left image, first copy the image you want to replace it with into the same folder that you copied the website template files to. Next, launch Composer if you have not already done so. (Recall that this involves starting the Mozilla Browser, and then going to the Window menu and choosing the Composer option.) Next, open the template's home page file, index.html, in Composer. This is accomplished by either clicking the Open icon in the toolbar or by going to the File menu and selecting the Open File menu option.

Once you have opened the index.html page in Composer, your screen should look similar to Figure 3.2.

To change the image of Sam to an image of your own, you'll need to open the Image

Properties dialog box for the image. This can be done in one of a number of ways: by right-clicking on the image and selecting the Image Properties menu option; by double-clicking the image; or by single-clicking the image and then clicking on the Image icon in the toolbar. Using any of these approaches will display the Image Properties dialog box (see Figure 3.3), from which you can customize the information about the displayed image.

The next section, "Specifying Image Properties," steps through the four tabs in the Image Properties dialog box and discusses how to replace the image of Sam with an image of your own. Keep in mind that you'll need to replace the image of Sam with your own image for each web page in the family/personal website template.

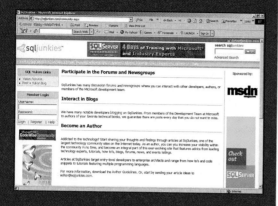

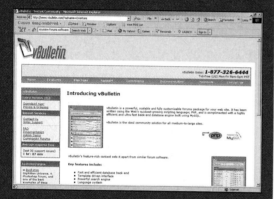

GREAT COMMUNITY SITE

If you're going to have a community website, then you have to tell people how to participate in your community. This site does a great job of telling visitors how they can interact with the rest of the community through blogs, discussion forums, newsgroups, and authoring articles.

If you click around their website, you'll find their discussion forum page that offers around 50 discussions. So how do you get a discussion page like that one? If you're reading this book, the best idea is to purchase discussion software from a company that has done all of the programming for you. VBulletin (www.vbulletin.com) is a pretty good discussion software that isn't too expensive—$85 annually for one server.

FIGURE 3.3
Customize the image from the Image Properties dialog box.

Specifying Image Properties

The Image Properties dialog box contains four tabs: Location, Dimensions, Appearance, and Link. These tabs contain settings to customize the selected image's properties. Let's look at each of these tabs one at a time.

The Location Tab

The Location tab, shown in Figure 3.3, allows you to specify the file to display. To change the upper-left image from one of my dog to one of your own, click on the Choose File button and select the image you want to display. Upon doing so, a small preview of the image selected will appear in the lower left corner of the Image Properties dialog box.

Next, from the Location tab, you can set the Alternate text for the image. This is the text that is displayed in the image's place for those visitors who are using text-only browsers or who have configured their browsers to not display images. Realistically, very few web surfers fall into this category, so feel free to simply not provide any alternate text. If you decide not to provide alternate text, be sure to select the Don't use alternate text radio button.

The Dimensions Tab

The next tab, Dimensions, allows you to customize the width and height of the image. As Figure 3.4 shows, the Dimensions tab has

two radio buttons: Actual Size and Custom Size. If you leave Actual Size selected, the image will be displayed in its actual size. If you click Custom Size, you can specify the image size in either pixels or as a percentage of the browser's window.

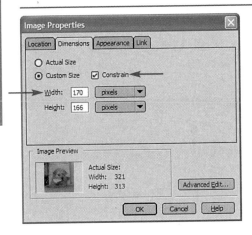

FIGURE 3.4
The image's size can be configured in the Dimensions tab.

The picture of Sam is scaled to a width of 170 pixels and a height of 166 pixels. As shown in the Image Preview section at the bottom of the dialog box in Figure 3.4, the actual image size is 321 pixels by 313 pixels.

Oftentimes an image will be resized so that it fits nicely on a page. The full-sized image of Sam is too large to fit nicely in the web page, hence it is scaled down to 170 by 166. When scaling images yourself, make sure to check the Constrain check box. This check box, if checked, makes sure that the ratio between the resized width and height remains the same as the original image's width and height ratio. By leaving this check box checked you ensure that resizing your image won't result in an image that is squished too fat or too thin.

When adding your own image, scale it so that it is at least 166 high. The family/personal website was designed to display an image precisely 166 pixels high. If you make the image shorter than 166 pixels, there will be whitespace beneath the image. When adding your own image, I would recommend that you

1. Select the Custom Size radio button.

2. Check the Constrain check box.

3. Enter 166 as the height.

NOTE

Realize that sizing the image smaller than its original size in the Dimensions tab only specifies to the browser to display the image as a certain size. Specifying a smaller size than the original does *not* reduce the image's file size. If you want to make the image a smaller file size, you need to use the resizing techniques discussed in the section "Resizing Digital Images," which can be found in the Bonus Chapter.

The Appearances Tab

The Appearances tab (shown in Figure 3.5) allows you to configure how the image will appear within text. The Spacing section lets you specify how much spacing should appear between the left and right and top and bottom of the image and the text around the image. The Solid Border text box permits you to specify whether the image should have a border and, if so, how many pixels wide it should be.

Additionally, you can choose how to have the text aligned with the image. You can have the following text appear at the bottom of the image, the center, or the top. Alternatively, you can have the image flow within the text on the left or right.

For the family/personal website, I'd recommend not changing the values in the Appearances tab, as the template was designed to have no spacing around the image.

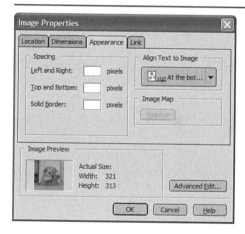

FIGURE 3.5

The Appearances tab specifies how the text and image coexist.

The Link Tab

The final tab, the Link tab, allows you to specify a hyperlink for the image. That is, you can indicate that when the image is clicked, the user be whisked to a particular URL. A screenshot of the Link tab is shown in Figure 3.6. See Table 3.1 for a summary of the Image Properties dialog box's tabs.

FIGURE 3.6

Use the Link tab to link the image to a URL.

TABLE 3.1	A Summary of the Image Properties Dialog Box's Tabs
Tab	**Description**
Location	Choose the image to display from the Location tab. You can provide a Tooltip, which will be displayed when a visitor hovers her mouse over the image. Also, the Location tab allows you to specify an Alternate text, which is displayed in place of the image for those visitors whose browsers don't support images.
Dimensions	From the Dimensions tab you can indicate a custom height and width for the image.
Appearance	The Appearance tab allows you to indicate the top, bottom, left, and right spacing around the image (if any), along with how text flows around the image.
Link	You can configure your image so that when a visitor clicks it he is whisked to a different web page. If you want to enable this behavior, specify the URL to send the user in the Link tab.

LOOKING FOR A WEB HOSTING SITE— SHOP AROUND

There are some great sites out there for hosting your website. We found SecureWebs to have a range of services and an online catalog of features. Shop around for the best deal and the types of services that you want. You may only need a small amount of space for a family or hobby website, which you can usually get from your Internet provider. Most accounts offer FTP access and a 50–100 MB of space for your own little website. But if you want to create a larger website, especially one that involves selling products or services, you might want to let a hosting site do most of the work for you. These sites take care of mass emailing, shopping carts, online catalogs, and newsletters for you. They also have security for your site, which can be difficult to program by yourself if you're a beginner. They have firewalls to prevent hackers from destroying your website as well as SSL (Secure Sockets Layer) that allows your visitors to perform transactions in a secure environment.

Removing the Image Altogether

While some readers will like having a picture shown on each page, others might not want a picture shown at all. Fortunately, Composer makes it a cinch to remove the image from the upper-left corner. To strike the image from the web page altogether, simply right-click on the image and choose the Delete menu option.

Changing the Font

The text in the web page templates is displayed using a Verdana font. You can easily change the font for any text in Composer with the following steps:

1. Select the text whose font you want to change. The easiest way to do this is to place the mouse at the beginning of the text you want to select, and, holding down the mouse button, drag the mouse cursor until the text you want to modify is completely selected.

2. With the text selected, go to the Format menu. Choose the Font menu option and then pick a font from the list.

You can also change other text properties—such as the text color and style—through the Format menu. For example, imagine that you wanted to change the foreground color of the header text for a web page. (The header text in the home page is "Welcome to the Mitchell Family Website!" and is displayed in a turquoise color.) To change this text's foreground color to, say, red, you'd first select the text and then go to the Format menu and choose the Text Color menu option. This will display the Text Color dialog box (see Figure 3.7), from which you can select a new foreground color.

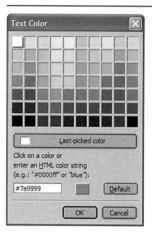

FIGURE 3.7

Pick the text's foreground color from the Text Color dialog box.

To make the font bold, italic, or underlined, first select the text and then go to the Format menu's Text Style menu. From there you can see the various formatting options.

> **TIP**
>
> To make the selected text bold, underline, or italic, you can also click on the appropriate B, I, or U icons in the toolbar.

Adding and Removing Pages from the Template

The family/personal website template comes with four web pages: a home page, a family pictures page, a recent events page, and a favorite recipes page. As we discussed earlier, though, you might very well want to add additional pages, or remove some of the pre-packaged pages.

Removing a page from the site simply entails removing the links from the other web pages to the page you wish to snip from the site. For example, imagine that you didn't want to have a favorite recipes page on your family/personal website. To accomplish this, you'd need to open the home page, family pictures page, and recent events page in Composer, and remove the link at the top to the Recent Events page. Removing the link is as simple as selecting the link text and hitting Delete.

NOTE

Keep in mind that you will need to remove *all* links to the page you want to remove. Be sure to open all other pages in Composer and remove any links you find pointing to the page to be removed.

To add a new page to the template, you need to create a new web page whose look and feel mimics that of the other pages in the template. Creating a new web page using the template can be done in one of two ways:

▸ By creating a new web page in Composer, and then copying and pasting the entire contents of a template page to the new page, or

▸ By going to the File menu and choosing the Save As menu option, which has the effect of saving an existing template web page with a different filename.

Once you have created the new web page and inherited the template's look and feel, you can customize the page's content as needed. For example, if you added an additional page that listed important dates for your family, the content for this page would include the dates and their meanings (anniversaries, birthdays, graduations, and so on). After you have created the content for the new page, save the web page by going to the File menu and choosing the Save menu option.

Once you have created and saved the new page, the next step is to add a link from all other web pages in the site to the new page. As Figure 3.1 showed, each page has a list of links along the top. You'll need to add a link up top to the new page you created.

To add a link, start by clicking your mouse where you want the link to appear, perhaps between the Family Pictures and Recent Events links. Next, type in the text for the link, such as "Important Dates", followed by a period, which is used as a separator between each link.

The final step is to link the text you just entered to the new web page you created. To accomplish this, select the text you just added, go to the Insert menu, and choose the Link menu option. This will display the Link Properties dialog box, shown in Figure 3.8.

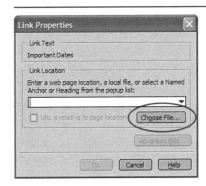

FIGURE 3.8

Select the page to link to using the Choose File button.

FINDING ADD-ONS FOR YOUR SITE

Cnet provides Downloads.com, which offers software that you can download, sometimes free of charge. The greatest thing about going to Cnet's site is that users rate the downloads, and you can view how many people have downloaded each program. You can find the most popular downloads, the top-rated downloads, and new releases. Why spend hours programming something for your website when you can download the component that you need? Here is a sampling of the kinds of tools you can find:

1 Cool Password Tool—Adds password protection to your site or a single page on your site without any program knowledge required.

Magic Gallery—Helps you create an online photo gallery.

DHTML Menu Builder—Creates DHTML drop-down menus for your site without you having to write the scripts.

Web CEO Free Edition—Get live traffic analysis of more than 160 reports with full coverage of your visitors' activity and e-commerce analysis.

Web Menus Studio 2005—Create professional-looking menus.

Forms To Go—Create custom scripts in PHP, ASP, or Perl to send the field values of your HTML forms thru email.

From the Link Properties dialog box, choose the file you want the user whisked to when they click the link. Since this link needs to take the user to the newly created page, click the Choose File button and select the page you added just a moment ago. Finally, click the OK button to create a hyperlink to the newly created page.

NOTE

Don't forget to add a link to the newly created page in all of the web pages in the site. If there are no links to the newly created page, then your visitors won't be able to get to the new page unless they manually enter the URL of the page in their browser's Address bar.

Customizing the Family Pictures Page

While family/personal websites are great for sharing recent events, recipes, and important dates, the main attraction to these types of websites is the family pictures. With digital cameras and scanners, it's incredibly easy to share pictures of your family, pets, vacations, and special events with friends and extended family.

"The family/personal website template contains a Family Pictures page where you can share your family's photographs with others."

The family/personal website template contains a Family Pictures page where you can share your family's photographs with others. In order to get started posting your pictures online, you will need to have the pictures you want to share in a digital format. If you own a digital camera, the photos stored on the camera are already in the needed format. If you want to put film pictures online, you have a couple options. If the picture already exists, you will need to get your hands on a *scanner*.

NOTE

A *scanner* is a piece of equipment that takes papers, pictures, or other flat documents, and makes a digital copy. Scanners are like copier machines, but rather than printing out a copy of the document being scanned, a scanner saves the image to a computer. Scanners are available at numerous stores like Best Buy, Circuit City, and so on, and can range in price from $50.00 to $500.00.

If you have taken pictures that you've yet to develop, you might be able to get the photographs developed as digital images. For an extra few bucks, you can get a CD of your pictures along with the developed photos.

NOTE

The Bonus Chapter has an in-depth discussion on digital images, including important digital imaging terminology and techniques for optimizing digital images.

Figure 3.9 shows a screenshot of the Family Pictures page, when viewed through Composer. Notice that the Family Pictures page contains a collage of pictures. Each image was added by going to the Insert menu and choosing the Image menu option. This will display the Image Properties dialog box, which we saw back in Figures 3.3 through 3.6. From the Image Properties dialog box, you can select the image you want to display and scale it accordingly. (All images shown on the Family Pictures page, for instance, were scaled so that they were no greater than 200 pixels wide or 200 pixels tall.)

In the next section, you'll see how you can add your own images to the Family Pictures page. Before you add your own pictures, though, you'll likely want to take a minute to remove those pictures included with the template. To accomplish this, open the Family Pictures page in Composer and select the image(s) you want to delete. Delete the selected image(s) by hitting the Delete button, or by going to the Edit menu and choosing the Delete menu option.

Adding New Images

Adding a new image to the Family Pictures web page involves two steps:

1. Copy the images from your digital camera or scanner to the same folder where you copied the template web pages.

2. Insert the image into the page via the Insert menu's Image menu option.

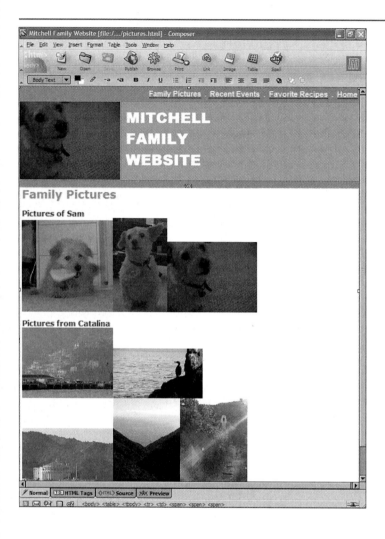

FIGURE 3.9

The Family Pictures page, when viewed in Composer.

Copying files from your digital camera or scanner differs on what brand of camera or scanner you have, so you'll have to refer to your camera or scanner's instructions to accomplish step 1. If you had your film developed into a CD, you'd just need to copy over the images from the CD to the appropriate folder.

Once the images have been copied over, open the Family Pictures page in Composer, if you

haven't already. To insert an image, go to the Insert menu and select the Image menu option (or, optionally, click the Image icon in the toolbar). This will display the Image Properties dialog box.

From the Locations tab (refer back to Figure 3.3), click the Choose File button and pick the image file you want to display. From the Dimensions tab (refer back to Figure 3.4), you can scale the image's height and width.

As Figure 3.9 shows, you can place images either side-by-side, or beneath one another. To place images side-by-side, simply insert one image right after the other. To create some space between the images, use the spacebar to add space on the same line, or hit the Enter key to have the image appear on the following line. You can also add spacing around the top, bottom, left, and right of an image through the Appearance tab (refer back to Figure 3.5).

NOTE

Make sure that the image file you add exists in the same folder as the web page. You'll see why this is important in the "Publishing Your Family/Personal Website" section, but for now realize that it is vital to having the image display properly for users visiting your website.

Publishing Your Family/Personal Website

At this point you have customized the web pages for the family/personal template, but these web pages still reside on your local computer, and are not accessible to others via the Internet. As discussed in Chapter 2, "Creating a Website," these files must be placed on a computer that has a dedicated connection to the Internet. Recall that there are a couple of steps you must go through to secure a public Internet website. Assuming you have completed these steps, publishing your Composer-created web pages is a breeze.

To publish a particular page, go to the File menu and choose Publish. This will display the Publish Page dialog box, which contains two

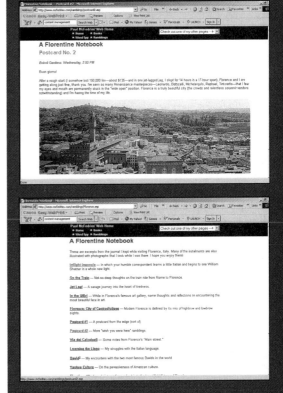

AWESOME PERSONAL JOURNAL

A great way to share vacation memories is to put your journal on your website. It doesn't have to be complicated. Just set up an index page and add entries as individual pages as you write them. Paul McFedries (one of Sams's authors) created a journal from his trip to Italy. The entries are fun to read and filled with pictures from his visit. He incorporated links to other entries or to whatever he was writing about for further information—a nice touch. This is a great site to study if you're looking for examples of good writing. Anyone can put vacation pictures on their website and tell friends what they did each day. But Paul's writing makes you feel like you're reading an insider's guide to Italy. His site is fun to read even if you don't know him.

tabs: Publish and Settings. As discussed in Chapter 2, the Settings tab allows you to specify information about the FTP server for the website as well as username and password information for the FTP server. You'll need to enter the FTP information provided by your web hosting provider in the Settings tab.

Once you have filled out the Settings tab, go to the Publish tab, which is shown in Figure 3.10. The Publish tab allows you to customize how the web page is published on the server. The default settings shown in Figure 3.10 are typically sufficient. To publish the web page, simply click the Publish button.

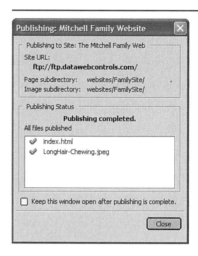

FIGURE 3.11

The index.html page has been published successfully!

Note that the dialog box in Figure 3.11 shows that two files have been uploaded to the web server—index.html and LongHair-Chewing.jpeg. What about the other web pages, such as pictures.html, events.html, and recipes.html? Those need to be uploaded too.

Unfortunately, with Composer you have to manually publish each of these files separately. That is, you need to open each file to publish in Composer, go to the File menu, and choose the Publish menu option.

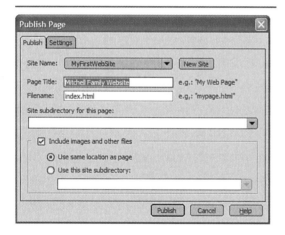

FIGURE 3.10

The Publish Page dialog box is used for publishing a web page to a public web server.

If the page is published successfully, you should see a dialog box like the one shown in Figure 3.11. This dialog box indicates the success or failure of publishing the web page and any associated files.

NOTE

Notice that when you publish a file to the web server, any image files in the web page are automatically published as well. For example, when the home page, index.html, is published, two files are uploaded to the web server: index.html and LongHair-Chewing.jpeg. The LongHair-Chewing.jpeg is the image file of Sam that is in the upper-left corner of the home page.

Placing Linked Files in the Same Folder

Throughout this chapter when adding hyperlinks to other web pages or image files, I have stressed the importance of placing the web pages or image files being linked to in the same folder as the page you are currently working on. If you do not do this, when a user visiting your site clicks on the link, they will not be taken to the desired page. Rather, they will see an error message informing them that the file requested could not be found.

Additionally, underneath the filename in the Link Properties dialog box there is an option called URL is relative to page location. When adding a link, this check box should be checked. After choosing a file by clicking the Choose File button, if the check box is unchecked, the text that appears in the drop-down list will look like file://pathToTheFile/FileName. If the check box is checked, the text in the drop-down list will have just the filename, and not the file://pathToTheFile/ prepended.

It is important that the file://pathToTheFile/ text does not appear before the file name. If it does, either uncheck the URL is relative to page location option, which will get rid of the offending text, or simply click on the text and delete the offending text manually.

You may be wondering why it is so important to have the URL is relative to page location check box checked. If you leave this unchecked, or leave in the file://pathToTheFile/ text, when the web page is published to the publicly available web server, these hyperlinks that were not successfully created will render as **broken links** in your visitor's web browsers.

"Be sure to check the URL is relative to page location check box for each hyperlink you create, and your hyperlinks will work properly for all web visitors."

A *broken link* is a hyperlink that, when clicked, displays an error informing the user that the web page cannot be found. The reason this error occurs is because for links created without URL is relative to page location checked, the hyperlink's URL is published as file://pathToTheFile/FileName, which is the path and filename on your desktop computer. When a user clicks this link, their web browser will see the file:// and will attempt to locate a file on their computer's hard drive located in the specified path and with the specified filename. This file will likely not exist on their computer, and, hence, they will get an error message informing them the file could not be found.

What is important to realize is that since the file exists on your computer, if you are testing your website from your computer, these links will render fine because you have these files on your computer! However, others will not be able to navigate through your website via these improperly created hyperlinks.

The short of it is, just be sure to check the URL is relative to page location check box for each hyperlink you create, and your hyperlinks will work properly for all web visitors.

Testing the Website

After you have published each web page for the family/personal website, take a moment to check out your website through a web browser. Launch your web browser and enter the URL to your website—in doing so you should see your family/personal website's home page.

Click around on the hyperlinks and make sure all pages are accessible. If you get an error message when clicking on a hyperlink chances are the error is due to one of the following two causes:

First, the error might have occurred because you forgot to publish the web page that the hyperlink was pointing to. Remember that *every* web page that you created with Composer must be published to the public website. So make sure that the web page you are having trouble accessing was, indeed, published (and published successfully).

If you are certain that the web page you are requesting has indeed been published, then the error might be due to a broken link. That is, the hyperlink you clicked on is directing the user to a URL of a web page that does not exist. This could be due to having created a hyperlink to an existing file, but then later changing the filename and not updating the hyperlink's URL. Also, it might be due to not having checked the URL is relative to page location check box in the Link Properties dialog box.

In either case, you'll need to reopen the web page that contains the offending link, fix the link problem, and republish the page.

Summary

Customizing a website template with Composer can be both fun and easy. The family/personal website template presented in this chapter had a home page and three

sections: a series of digital photographs, the latest family news, and favorite family recipes. As you saw, customizing the existing pages— changing the text content, altering the colors, selecting a different font or formatting, and so on—are all very easy to accomplish with Composer. You can edit a web page just like you would edit a document with a word processor program.

In addition to working with the provided template web pages, you are encouraged to add additional pieces to your family/personal website so that the site is customized for you and your family. As discussed in this chapter, to add new pages you start by creating a new web page with the layout as another page in your template. From there, you can customize the new page's content. After this, all that remains is to update the other pages so that they provide a hyperlink to the newly created page.

In addition to customizing the template, we looked at how to publish the template to a web server once the customizations had been completed. To publish your web pages, you need to load each web page in Composer and choose the Publish menu option from the File menu. Publishing your web page will upload the actual web page along with any images displayed in the page. Once all of your web pages have been uploaded to the website, anyone with an Internet connection can view your site through a browser!

CHAPTER 4

Creating a Hobby Website

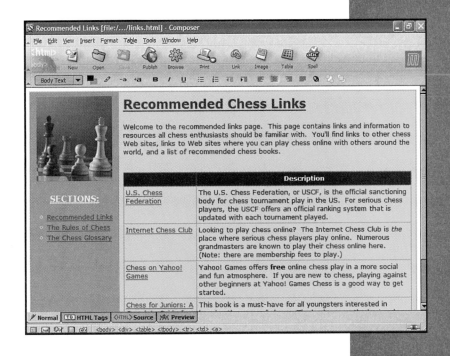

Many people participate in one or more hobbies they thoroughly enjoy. Prior to the Internet, the only way to get in touch with others who might enjoy the same hobby was to join or start some sort of local club. For example, where I live there are groups that

- Meet weekly to dance
- Get together on the weekends to play games like chess, bridge, and others
- Go out to the mountains once a month to do day-long hikes
- Form leagues to play various sports, like football, soccer, basketball, and so on

Today, the Internet offers another medium by which you can share your hobby with others and meet individuals who also participate in the hobby. Due to the global reach of the Internet, these individuals might be your next door neighbors or people halfway around the world.

In this chapter, we will examine the hobby website template that is included in the accompanying CD.

Examining the Hobby Website Template

Hobby websites typically contain the following set of pages:

- A home page that gives a brief description of the hobby with links to the other sections of the site.

- A page that lists recommended links. Recommended links are links to websites that you think the average hobby enthusiast will find useful. These can be links to books on Amazon.com, links to other websites about the same hobby, and so on.
- A page that provides a detailed description of the hobby, such as the rules, etiquette, and history of the hobby.

In addition to these standard pages, there are additional web pages that you can easily add to the hobby website template. Other common hobby web pages include

- A glossary page, providing definitions of relevant terms.
- Information on local clubs or groups that partake in the hobby.
- Information about your participation in the hobby. Perhaps a bit on how you got started with the hobby, if you are part of any clubs or organizations that participate in the hobby, and so on.
- If you have been involved in the particular hobby for quite some time, you can likely give some good tips and advice to those who may not have had as much experience as you.

The template in the accompanying CD provides a hobby site for chess enthusiasts (see Figure 4.1). It is composed of four separate web pages: a home page, a page of recommended links, a discussion of the rules of chess, and a chess glossary. Using the template, you can easily add additional pages with minimal effort.

FIGURE 4.1

The hobby website template.

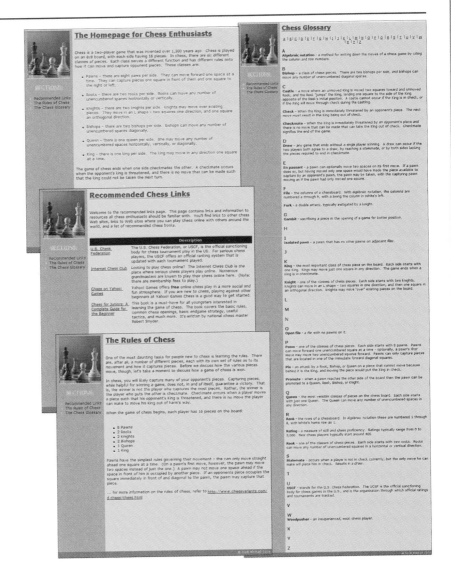

The chess site's home page gives a brief description of the game of chess in the right column, with the site's various sections listed in the left column. The three sections for this site include

▶ A list of recommended links. This includes links to other chess hobby websites and recommended chess books and articles.

▶ The rules of chess. A detailed listing of the rules of chess are provided for those who are new to the hobby.

▸ A chess glossary. The glossary contains an alphabetized list of chess terms, along with their definitions.

The remainder of this chapter looks at how to customize the template for creating a website suited to your particular hobby. You'll see how easy it is to add additional web pages to the hobby site template. The chapter wraps up by looking at how to publish your customized hobby website to a web server, so others can visit your site.

Customizing the Template

When creating your own hobby website, you'll no doubt want to customize the provided template to suit your hobby and aesthetic tastes. For example, the chess site contains an image of chess pieces in the upper-left corner of every page. Unless you are creating a chess hobby site yourself, you'll likely want to change this image to one that's more appropriate for your particular hobby.

"As discussed earlier, hobby websites can have a variety of accompanying web pages. The template includes four pages. If you want to add additional pages—such as a page that lists local groups and clubs that participate in the hobby—you'll need to create a new web page that has the same look and feel of all the other template web pages."

You might also want to change the color scheme of the template. The provided template uses a brown color scheme with varying shades of brown as the background colors for the left and right columns, and another shade of brown for the text color. With just a few clicks of the mouse, though, you can customize the color scheme to meet your own tastes.

As discussed earlier, hobby websites can have a variety of accompanying web pages. The template includes four pages. If you want to add additional pages—such as a page that lists local groups and clubs that participate in the hobby—you'll need to create a new web page that has the same look and feel of all the other template web pages. This is an easy task taking only a few minutes.

Changing the Upper-Left Image

Each page in the template contains an image of chess pieces in the upper-left corner. This image, when clicked, will whisk the user back to the hobby site's main page (**index.html**). While the picture of chess pieces fits in nicely with a hobby site dedicated to the game of chess, when customizing this template to create your own hobby website, you would likely want to use an image more suited to your hobby.

Before changing the chess pieces image, you'll first need to locate an image you want to place there instead. This might be a photo of people participating in your selected hobby, for example. One option is to take a picture yourself with a digital camera. Another option is to search the web for suitable images using Google's Image Search—**http://images.google.com**.

NOTE

Images returned by Google's Image Search might be copyrighted images. Be sure to get permission from the creator of the image before posting the image on your own, public website.

Once you have located or created a suitable image, copy it to the same directory where you've saved the hobby website's template pages. To replace the image of the chess pieces, follow these steps:

1. Open the Image Properties dialog box. This can be done by either double-clicking on the image of the chess pieces, or by single-clicking on the image of the chess pieces and selecting the Insert menu's Image menu option.

2. The Image Properties dialog box contains four tabs: Location, Dimensions, Appearance, and Link (see Figure 4.2). Navigate to the Location tab.

3. From the Location tab, you can specify the file to display in the image. As Figure 4.2 shows, the file being displayed in the template is chess.jpg. To load your own image here, click on the Choose File button and browse to the image you want to include.

NOTE

When adding an image file to a web page in Composer, make sure that the image file is in the same folder as the web page file itself. Also, when adding an image through the Image Properties dialog box, make sure that the "URL is relative to page location" check box is checked.

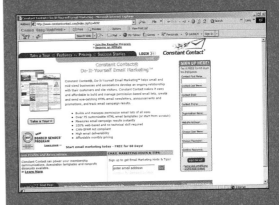

NEWSLETTERS 101

Depending on the type of website you develop, you may want to send email newsletters to people who register on your site. There are all kinds of things to consider when you're going to build a list and email people.

1) How many email blasts can I send from my Internet provider? Is there a limit?

2) How do I prevent my messages from being filtered as spam?

3) How do I know if people are even opening my messages?

4) Should I create text-based messages or HTML messages?

5) What is the most effective way to communicate with people via email?

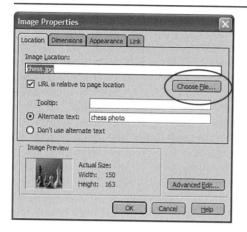

FIGURE 4.2

Specify the image to display from the Location tab.

From the Location tab, you can also provide Alternate Text for the image. The Alternate Text is useful for users who are visiting your site with a browser that doesn't support images, such as Braille browsers used by the blind.

Scaling the Image

The hobby website template is designed to display an upper-left corner image that is no wider than 150 pixels. If you have added an image whose width is greater than 150 pixels, it will cause the left column to expand to the width of the image, thereby squishing the text in the right column.

NOTE

A *pixel* is the base unit of measurement for a digital image. A single pixel represents a point in a digital image. The more pixels wide and tall an image is, the taller and wider it is on the screen. For more information on digital images, be sure to read the Bonus Chapter.

If the image you are adding is greater than 150 pixels wide, you can scale it through the Image Properties dialog box's Dimensions tab. Through the Dimensions tab you can indicate whether the image should be displayed in its actual width, or whether it should be scaled to a custom size. If the image is too wide, be sure to opt to have it scaled to a width of 150 pixels, as shown in Figure 4.3.

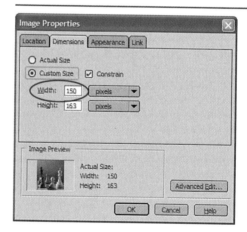

FIGURE 4.3

Large images need to be scaled so that they are no wider than 150 pixels.

If you decide to change the image you'll need to do so in all of the web pages in the template.

Changing the Color Scheme

The hobby website template uses a brown color scheme. The left and right columns' backgrounds are differing shades of brown, and the text in the right column is a shade of brown as well. If you do not like this color scheme, you can easily change it to something that better fits your tastes.

To change the background color of either the left or right columns, right-click in the appropriate column and choose the Table of Cell Background Color menu option. This will display the Table or Cell Color dialog box (see Figure 4.4), from which you can select the background color to use.

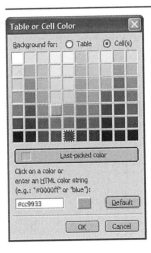

FIGURE 4.4

Choose a background color from the Table or Cell Color dialog box.

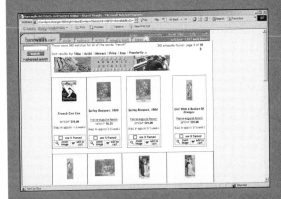

THE ART OF NAVIGATION

Shopping on the web is easy if the site you're visiting offers different ways to browse their products. Barewalls.com lets you find their artwork in a variety of ways—by style, by subject, by artist. They also categorize artwork into museum art, contemporary art, pop culture, and photography. Once you click on a category, you can sort your choices by popularity, size, price, and so on. This site knows how to exploit its advantages over brick and mortar art galleries and other art websites that don't offer such a variety of ways to find artwork.

If you're planning an ecommerce website, think about ways that customers will want to search your site. Make it as easy as possible for them to find the right products.

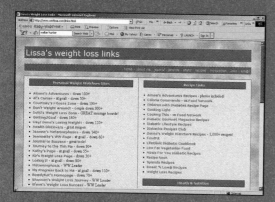

Lissa's weight loss links

SIMPLE IS GOOD

What's so great about Lissa's Weight Loss page? It's simple. We love this site because it has everything you'd ever want to find about one thing—weight loss. The first page is a jumping off place for just about everything you might need—other people's personal weight loss sites, recipe links, health and nutrition links, fitness and exercise, newsgroups, and weight loss calculators. Each category has a bulleted list of links. That's it.

We've seen other sites that offer plenty of information, but why bother visiting when the pages are so complicated and busy that you can't find what you want? You've seen those kinds of sites—different font sizes all over the place, pictures everywhere, flashing images, and an obnoxious array of colors.

So what's the lesson? Your site doesn't have to be fancy or beautiful to be great. Fill it with content that people want and make it easy for them to find things—that's it.

To change the foreground color of the text in the right column, simply follow these steps:

1. Start by selecting the text whose color you want to change. Selecting text in Composer is just like selecting text in a word processor program—move your mouse to the beginning of the text to select, hold down the left mouse button, and drag the mouse, selecting the appropriate text.

2. Once you have selected the text, you can set the text's foreground color by going to the Format menu and selecting the Text Color menu option. This will display the Text Color dialog box, which looks just like the Table or Cell Color dialog box shown in Figure 4.4.

3. To change the text's foreground color, simply select a color from the Text Color dialog box and click OK.

TIP

If you choose a light background color, be sure that the web page text is a dark color. Likewise, if you choose a dark background color, you should use a light text color. If you fail to choose contrasting foreground and background colors, the text on your web page will be hard to read.

Adding and Removing Pages from the Template

The hobby website template comes with four web pages: a home page, a list of recommended links, the rules of chess, and a chess glossary. When customizing the template for your website you might want to remove some of these pages, or add additional pages.

Fortunately, making such customizations is a simple process, taking only a few minutes to complete.

To remove a page from the template, all that you need to do is remove the links to that page from all other pages in the template. For example, imagine that you did not want a glossary page. To remove this from your customized hobby website, you'd only need to go to the remaining three pages—the home page, recommended links page, and rules page—and remove the link to the glossary from the left column.

To add a new page to the template, you need to create a new web page whose look and feel mimics that of the other pages in the template. As we saw in Chapter 3, "Creating a Family/Personal Website," creating a new web page using the template can be done in one of two ways:

▶ By creating a new web page in Composer, and then copying and pasting the entire contents of a template page to the new page.

▶ By going to the File menu and choosing the Save As menu option, which has the effect of saving an existing template web page with a different filename.

Once you have created the new web page and inherited the template's look and feel, you can customize the page's content as needed. For example, if you added an additional page that listed clubs or organizations in your area that participate in the hobby (such as local chess clubs), the content for this page would likely be a listing of the clubs, the dates and times they meet, and links to their websites.

After you have created the content for the new page, save the web page by going to the File menu and choosing the Save menu option. Next, you'll need to add a link to this newly created page in each other page in the site.

To add a link in the left-hand column, place the cursor at the end of the last link (The Chess Glossary) and hit Enter. This will start a new item in the bulleted list. Next, type in the name of the newly created page that you want to link to, such as Local Chess Clubs. Finally, you need to link the text you just entered to the appropriate web page. To accomplish this, select the text and then go to the Insert menu, selecting the Link menu option. This will display the Link Properties dialog box (see Figure 4.5). From the Link Properties dialog box, use the Choose File button to browse to the new web page that you added earlier.

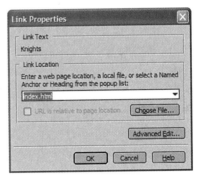

FIGURE 4.5

Select the page to link to using the Choose File button.

NOTE

Be sure to add a link to the newly created page in all of the web pages in the site. If there are no links to the newly created page, then your visitors won't be able to get to the new page unless they manually enter the URL of the page in their browser's Address bar.

Customizing the Recommended Links Page

An important part to any hobby site is information on how the visitor can learn more about the hobby or become active in the hobby. This can include links to other, related hobby websites; book recommendations; and links or descriptions of other resources. The hobby website template contains a Recommended Links page with links to online chess tutorials, websites where individuals can play one another online, and recommended books.

When customizing the template for your personal hobby site, you'll likely want to replace the Recommended Links provided in the template with your own recommended links. Also, you might want to add more than four recommended links. In this section, we'll see how to change the existing four recommended links as well as how to add new recommended links.

Editing the Template's Recommended Links

The template displays the recommended links in a two-column table. The left column provides a short description for the link. The right column gives a much more detailed description of the recommended link.

To edit one of the recommended links, you'll need to do three things:

1. Change the text of the link in the left column.

2. Change the URL the link refers to in the left column.

3. Change the description in the right column.

Imagine that you decided to create a hobby site about basketball. You might want to change the first recommended link in the template, titled U.S. Chess Federation and pointing to http://www.uschess.org/, to a link to the National Basketball Association's home page (www.NBA.com). To accomplish this you'd do the following three things:

1. First change the link's text from U.S. Chess Federation to Official NBA Web Site.

2. Next, you'd need to change the link from http://www.uschess.org/ to http://www.nba.com/ by either double-clicking the hyperlink or by selecting the text, going to the Insert menu, and choosing the Link menu option. Either set of steps would display the Link Properties dialog box, from which you could type in http://www.nba.com/.

3. Finally, you'd want to change the associated description in the right column. The description might contain a sentence or two about what information could be found at NBA.com.

These three steps would need to be repeated for each recommended link that you wanted to edit.

Adding New Recommended Links

Creating a new link in the Recommended Links page begins with adding a new row to the table that contains the links. Once a new row has been inserted, you can add the link in the left column and the description in the right column.

There are two ways to add a new row to a table with Composer. The first is to place the cursor in the last cell (the rightmost, bottommost cell). Then, hit the Tab key. This will automatically create a new row at the end of the table, and place the cursor in the first column of the new row.

The second means to add a new to a table offers more control over where the new row is inserted. To utilize this approach, right-click on the table row above or below where you want to add the new row. Right-clicking will display a context menu, with one of the choices being Table Insert. The Table Insert option contains a number of options, the two of interest being Row Above and Row Below. Select either one of these to add the new row above or below the current selected row.

Once you have added the new row, the next step is to add the link in the left column and the description in the right column.

To add the link start by typing in the link's title in the left column. Once you have accomplished this, select the text, go to the Insert menu, and choose the Link menu option. This will display the Link Properties dialog box from which you can specify the URL the link should direct the user to. To add the description, simply type in the link's description in the right column.

When adding the link and description, you will notice that the font size and color of the newly added link and description do not match the size and color of the other links in the table. To tweak the font size and color start by selecting the newly added text. To set its color, go to the Format menu and choose the Text Color menu option. (The template uses the dark brown palette color in the second column of the bottommost row, HTML color string #330000.) To reduce the font size, either click on the toolbar icon "–a" to shrink the font size (see Figure 4.6), or go to the Format menu, choose Size, and select the Smaller menu item.

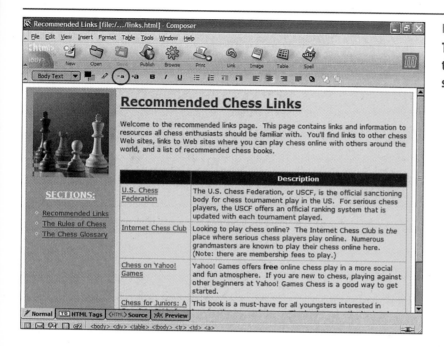

FIGURE 4.6
The –a icon will reduce
the selected text's font
size.

Editing the Glossary

Chess is a rather intricate game, with many rules, special moves, strategies, and concepts. For those individuals new to the game, a glossary will provide a quick way for them to look up terms they encounter on the website, on other chess-related sites, or in a book. Depending on the hobby website you create, you may or may not need a glossary page. If you do, you'll only need to edit the glossary items so that the terms it provides are pertinent to your hobby. (You'll learn how to edit the glossary in this section.) If you do not need a glossary, you can remove this page from the template using the techniques discussed in the "Adding and Removing Pages from the Template" section in this chapter.

The glossary page provides an arbitrary number of terms, ordered alphabetically. As Figure 4.7 shows, the glossary page contains the letters of the alphabet in two places:

▶ Listed down the page. Here each letter is listed as an *anchor*. Think of an anchor as a saved spot in a page that the user can be automatically sent to. Under each letter are the terms that begin with that letter. For example, under the letter A is the term "Algebraic notation."

▶ Listed along the top of the page. Here, each letter of the alphabet is listed as a link. Each letter is linked to the appropriate anchor. When the user clicks on one of these letters along the top, their browser will automatically scroll to the appropriate letter, showing those terms that begin with that letter.

FIGURE 4.7

The letters of the alphabet run down the side, with the appropriate terms listed underneath.

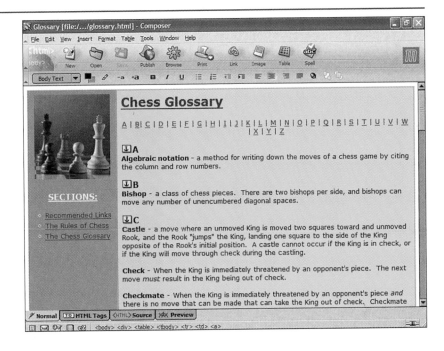

The glossary page already contains all of the anchors and links that you'll need. To customize the glossary page, all you need to do is delete those terms you don't need, and add the terms pertinent to your hobby under the correct letter of the alphabet.

NOTE

When inspecting the screenshot in Figure 4.7, or viewing the web page in Composer, you likely will notice the anchor icon next to each letter of the alphabet running down the page. Don't worry, the anchor icon will *not* appear in a visitor's web browser when they are visiting this web page. The icon is displayed only by Composer to indicate that a named anchor has been placed at that location.

Publishing the Hobby Website

In order to make your chess hobby website available to others via the Internet, you'll need to publish your web pages to a publicly available website, just like you did with the family/personal website you created in the previous chapter. As discussed in the "Publishing Your Family/Personal Website" section in the previous chapter, to publish the website you need to open each web page for the site, go to the File menu, and choose the Publish menu option.

We won't discuss the details of publishing the hobby website here, as the steps are the same as the ones discussed in the previous chapter.

THINK LIKE A CUSTOMER

West Elm is a contemporary home furnishing site that offers more than attractive home furniture. It offers the user a shopping experience similar to one they would have at an actual store with one advantage—users can go directly to the item they are interested in purchasing without going through the entire store. The site is organized by item, such as sofas, accessories, and so on, or you can shop by room, such as living room, office, and so forth. It is quite simple in its design, offering a clean, clear way to shop for home furnishings. Selected items can be displayed in a larger format or in your chosen color, taking the guesswork out when looking only at a color swatch. The site is very usable, which is important to keep in mind when designing a site. Simply, the easier navigation is, the cleaner your design makes a better experience for your visitor. Making things complex when they don't need to be only frustrates your visitor. And most often the goal is repeat visitors, so providing a pleasant experience at first click is an important goal for any website designer.

For a more detailed discussion of publishing the hobby website, refer back to the "Publishing Your Family/Personal Website" section in Chapter 3.

Summary

In this chapter, we examined how to customize the hobby website template, which is a breeze using Composer. You saw how to change the upper-left image in each page of the template, for example, by double-clicking the image and selecting a different image file. You also learned how to customize the content in the recommended links and glossary pages.

Adding or removing web pages from the template is also possible. As discussed, removing a page from the template is as simple as removing those hyperlinks to it from the other pages in the website. To add a new page, you create a new web page in Composer that has the same layout as the other template pages. This new page's content can then be customized. The last step is to add links to the new page from the other pages in the site.

Creating your own hobby website can be fun and rewarding for both you and others. They are a great way to share your avocation with others. With the global reach of the Internet, your hobby, expertise, and enjoyment can be shared with others from around the world.

CHAPTER 5

Creating a Website for an Organization

Just about everybody who has a computer these days has access to the Internet. As you saw in the previous two chapters, the pervasiveness of the Internet allows for distant friends and family to stay in touch, as well as an opportunity for individuals who enjoy a common hobby to come together. Clearly the Internet offers the ability for distant people to share information, but the Internet is also useful for sharing information among local individuals.

If you are active in any government committees, such as a city council, or are involved in any clubs or organizations, such as the Rotary Club, the Knights of Columbus, or a local book club, then you know part of the challenge of such organizations is providing information to its members.

Prior to the Internet, this information was typically distributed via printed newsletters, mentions in the town newspaper, or by old-fashioned word of mouth. With the Internet, however, many organizations—especially government organizations—are placing this information online. By making this information available via the Internet, the club's members can stay abreast of the events and news, and prospective members can learn more about the organization and its upcoming schedule.

In this chapter, you'll examine a template for creating an organization's website. You can customize this template to create a website for any organizations with which you're involved.

Examining the Organization Website Template

Websites for organizations typically serve to disseminate information about the organization to both its current members and prospective members. This information might include

- Upcoming events and activities
- Meeting dates and schedules
- A current list of members
- The minutes from previous meetings
- The board members or leaders of the organization, and their contact information
- General information about the organization, such as its mission statement or purpose

The organization website template included with this book's CD offers a template for a fictional botanical club in San Diego, California (see Figure 5.1). The template contains three web pages: a home page, information about meeting dates (including a map of the meeting location), and a member list.

NOTE

Organizational websites are very common among agencies at all levels of government, providing important information to the citizenry. Chances are your local government has organizational websites for various councils and bureaus.

FIGURE 5.1
The organization website template.

Customizing the Template

The organization website template uses a number of images specific to the botanical club site. For example, at the top of each page are three photographs of flowers, which are fitting for a botanical club's website, but might not be for your organization's site. Also, on the Meeting Dates page, there is a map of the meeting location. When customizing this template, you'll likely want to change the top images as well as the map image. We'll discuss how to accomplish this in the "Customizing the Images" section.

The provided template is rather simple, consisting of only three web pages. If you have a large or active organization, chances are you'll want much more information up on the website, such as instructions on how to become a member, the minutes from the last meeting, and so on. You'll also learn how to easily add new pages to the template.

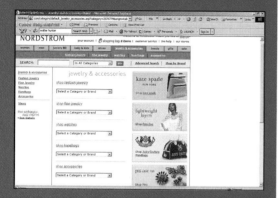

WHAT MAKES YOUR SITE STAND OUT FROM THE CROWD? WHY TO INVEST IN SEARCHING AND BROWSING

This site is a good one to review when you have lots of items or information to display. This major retailer has thousands of items that are organized under many categories. Those categories are then broken into subcategories, which provide easier site navigation. The items are often under more than one category, offering the user an efficient way to get to the same item. For instance, this site touts itself as the world's biggest shoe store. As you can imagine, that is a lot of shoes, and can be daunting when you are looking for something specific like loafers or boots. The intuitive organization offers categories such as Women's, Men's, Kids, and brands at the first level, but then Women's is broken down into 20 categories, ranging from flats to wedding shoes. More timesaving categories allow you to search by price, brand, bestseller, or "what's new." Of course, if you have the time, you can certainly click on "search all", and review every style, price, brand, and color! Providing the right categories is important when dealing with lots of items, as visitors can quickly they can find what they are looking for and will most likely result in additional visits to your site.

Customizing the Images

As Figure 5.1 shows, the organization website template contains a row of three pictures of flowers at the top of each page. These pictures improve the aesthetics of the site, and are fitting since the site is for a botanical club. In customizing the template for your organization's site, though, you might want to replace those images with your own. Using your own images on the website is as simple as following these steps:

1. The first step in this process is getting your hands on the image files that you want to use on your site. These can be pictures taken from a digital camera, or created through a graphics program such as Adobe Photoshop. The organization website template was designed to hold three images each 250 pixels wide and 200 pixels tall, so make sure you resize the image you want to use to 250x200. Once you have the properly sized image files, you'll need to copy them to the same folder that you placed the website template files in.

2. Next, to replace one of the flower images with your custom image, open one of the template web pages in Composer and then double-click on the image you want to change. This will display the Image Properties dialog box, as shown in Figure 5.2.

3. From the Location tab, you can click the Choose File button to select your custom image file. (Again, it should be in the same folder as the web page file.)

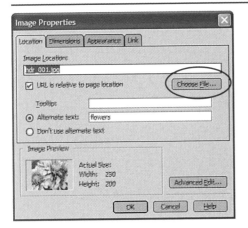

FIGURE 5.2

Choose the image file to display by clicking on the Choose File button.

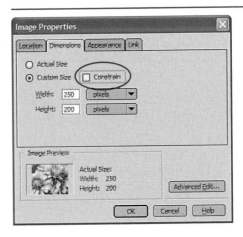

FIGURE 5.3

Use the Dimensions tab to ensure that the image is 250x200.

If the new image you added is precisely 250x200, then you are done at this point. If, however, the image is not exactly that dimension, you'll need to navigate to the Dimensions tab. From the Dimensions tab, select the Custom Size radio button, uncheck the Constrain check box, and then enter the Width as 250 pixels, and the Height as 200 pixels (see Figure 5.3).

Upon properly sizing the image, click the OK button. This will return you to Composer, having your custom image in place of the default flower image. Repeat this process for all three images on this page, as well as all three images on all of the template's pages.

Adding a Map of the Meeting Location

Figure 5.4 shows a screenshot of the Meeting Dates page when viewed through a browser. Along with sharing the meeting dates, this web page should also inform members and potential members where the organization meets. While this information can be provided by simply giving a street address, it is helpful to also show a map of the meeting location.

To add a map to a web page, the simplest approach is to use one of the map service sites, such as **http://maps.yahoo.com**, **http://www.mapquest.com**, and **http://www.mappoint.com**. These sites allow you to enter a street address and will display a corresponding map at a specified level of detail. To add a map of your organization's headquarters or meeting location follow these simple four steps:

78

FIGURE 5.4

The Meeting Dates page has a map of the meeting location.

1. Navigate to one of these map service websites and enter the address you need a map for. You will be shown a map that you can save and add to your web page.

2. To save the generated map, right-click on the map and choose to save the image. Be sure to save the image in the same folder that contains the website template files.

3. Once you have saved the map, you can then add the map to the web page by going to the Insert menu and choosing the Image menu option. This will display the Image Properties dialog box (refer back to Figure 5.2).

4. Click the Choose File button and select the map file you just saved. The map will then be displayed in the web page.

Customizing the Contact Us Link

Each of the three web pages in the template contains a Contact Us hyperlink in the right column. This hyperlink, when clicked, does not direct the visitor to some other URL; rather, it automatically opens their email program and starts a new email message addressed to club@greenthumb.com. You'll want to change this link so that, when clicked, the visitor will begin writing an email addressed to you.

To make this customization, either double-click the Contact Us text, or select the Contact Us text and choose the Insert menu's Link menu option. Either way will display the Link Properties dialog box, which is shown in Figure 5.5.

FIGURE 5.5
The Link Properties dialog box for the Contact Us hyperlink.

Notice that the Link Location value contains not just the email address, but also mailto:. When creating a hyperlink that, when clicked, should start composing an email message rather than whisk the user to a new URL, the

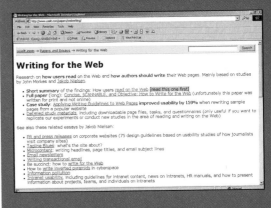

WRITING FOR YOUR SITE

"The most valuable of all talents is that of never using two words when one will do."
—Thomas Jefferson

Writing for the Web by Jakob Nielson is an older website, but still offers very relevant information about writing styles and effective communications with people. Although not the most attractive page, Jakob leads you to articles and other places to reference style rules, usability studies, guidelines for writing different kinds of text such as newsletters and press releases, as well as tips on writing headlines, subjects, and page titles that will get people's attention.

hyperlink's Link Location must be prefixed with mailto:. For example, if you wanted a user to begin composing an email to you@you.com when they clicked a link, you'd set the link's Link Location to mailto:you@you.com.

NOTE

Each of the three pages in the organization website template contains a Contact Us hyperlink with a Link Location of mailto:club@greenthumb.com. Before publishing your site, be sure to change this Link Location on all pages so that when a visitor clicks the Contact Us button they're sending an email to your email address, and not club@greenthumb.com.

Adding Additional Pages to the Template

The organization website template comes with three web pages: a home page, a Meeting Dates page, and a Member Directory page. When customizing the template for your website, you might want to add additional pages to provide additional information about your organization. These added pages might include meeting minutes, instructions on how to become a member, or a page providing the organization's charter and bylaws.

"To add a new page to the template, you need to create a new web page whose look and feel mimics that of the other pages in the template."

To add a new page to the template, you need to create a new web page whose look and feel mimics that of the other pages in the template. As we saw in both Chapters 3 and 4, creating a new web page using the template can be done in one of two ways:

▸ By creating a new web page in Composer, and then copying and pasting the entire contents of a template page to the new page.

▸ By going to the File menu and choosing the Save As menu option, which has the effect of saving an existing template web page with a different filename.

Once you have created the new web page and inherited the template's look and feel, you can customize the page's content as needed. For example, if you added an additional page that listed instructions for potential members on how to join, the content for this page would likely contain the application to join, information about dues and member requirements, and other pertinent information.

After you have created the content for the new page, save the web page by going to the File menu and choosing the Save menu option. Next, you'll need to add a link to this newly created page in the right column on each other page in the site.

To add a link in the right column, place the cursor where you want the new link to appear (perhaps between the Member Directory and Contact Us links). Next, type in the name of the newly created page that you want to link to, such as Join Our Club. Finally, you need to link the text you just entered to the appropriate web page. To accomplish this, select the text and then go to the Insert menu, selecting the Link menu option. This will display the Link Properties dialog box. From here use the Choose File button to browse to the new web page that you added earlier.

> **NOTE**
>
> Remember that links serve as the means for visitors to move from one web page to another. For this reason, be sure to add a link to the newly created page in all of the web pages in the site, so that visitors can reach the new page from any other.

Publishing the Website

Once you have completed the customization of the organization website template, you're ready to publish the site to a publicly available web server. Recall that this is accomplished by publishing each of the web pages by going to the File menu and choosing the Publish menu option. Open each of the web pages and publish them one at a time. When you're done you should be able to access the website via the public web server you uploaded the pages to.

> **NOTE**
>
> For a more thorough description on publishing your website, refer back to the "Publishing Your Family/Personal Website" section in Chapter 3, "Creating a Family/Personal Website."

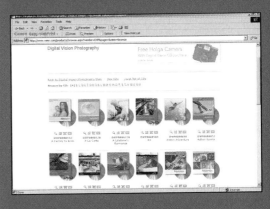

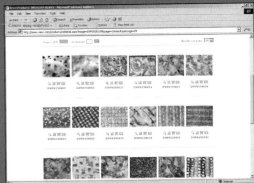

FONTS, IMAGES, PHOTOS, AND ILLUSTRATIONS FOR YOUR SITE

What if you want beautiful photos or illustrations for your site, but you're not an artist? Veer.com and plenty of other stock image sites offer great deals on images.

We liked Veer because they also print catalogs and offer them in PDF format from their website. Their catalogs are works of art themselves and can give you some great ideas for how to use images and type.

Here are a couple of tips to remember when looking for a stock image:

1. Royalty-free images are your best buy.

2. If you want the same look to your website, buy a CD of images that were designed to go together.

ADS ON YOUR SITE?

What if your site becomes pretty popular? You might want to consider putting ads, like Google Ads, on your site to bring extra revenue. Google's AdSense delivers advertising that is targeted to customers who like your content. You receive revenue any time a visitor from your site clicks through to one of the ads in the Google sidebar. Google ads are tastefully done—no big flashing ads or pop-ups that annoy your visitors.

There are tons of ways to make money from your website even if you don't sell anything. Check out the site called Web Marketing Today (http://www.wilsonweb.com/wmta/adrev-8steps.htm).

Summary

In this chapter, you examined how to customize the organizational website template. When creating a website for an organization, be certain to provide pertinent information for both existing members and prospective members, such as current members, information about the last meeting, and so on.

While the provided template only contains three web pages in total, it's easy to add additional pages when customizing the template. When crafting your organization's website, ask yourself what sort of information needs to be shared, as these bits of information make great additions to the website. Perhaps your organization already has some bits of information regularly committed to print, such as meeting minutes, or a newsletter.

As you saw in this chapter, adding new content to the organizational website template is a snap with Composer. Simply create a new web page with the template's layout, add the content, and place links to the new page on the other pages in the site. With this technique you can quickly add additional pages to your organization's website.

You also learned how to add a map to a web page. If your organization has a regular meeting location or a headquarters or central office, a map can prove helpful.

In the next chapter, "Creating an Informational Website for Your Business," you'll see how to utilize the Internet as another form of advertising. Specifically, we'll look at how a business can provide information about its products and services through a website as an additional and affordable means of reaching existing and potential customers.

CHAPTER 6

Creating an Informational Website for Your Business

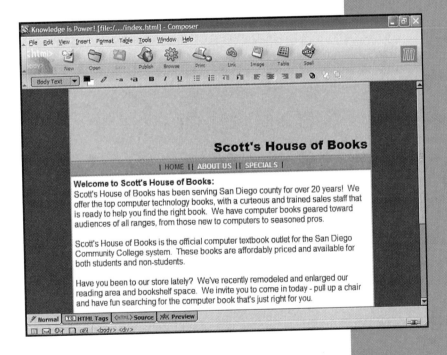

When I bought a car earlier in the year, I began my research by visiting various local car dealers' websites. I knew the type of car I was interested in—a four-dour sedan, either a Honda or Toyota—and just needed to find the car that had the features I needed for the price I was willing to pay. Visiting the websites of local car dealerships I was able to quickly find out what special sales they had going, the prices for various makes and models, what features were included and what would cost extra (and how much extra), as well as financing options. With a connection to the Internet, I was able to research my options without having to spend a Saturday visiting multiple car dealerships and shooing away overzealous car salesmen.

"Multiple studies have shown that more and more consumers are turning to the Internet as a means for researching products before buying."

Multiple studies have shown that more and more consumers are turning to the Internet as a means for researching products before buying. For businesses, these studies highlight the importance of having a website that showcases the products and services offered. When searching for a car, I only researched car dealerships that had a web presence. Hence, if a car dealership lacked a website, they were not in the running for my business.

There's no reason a business should not have a web presence in today's digital age. With the increasing numbers of online-savvy customers, businesses without a website are simply turning away potential customers. All businesses, both large and small, can benefit from a web presence.

This chapter presents an informational website template for a fictional bookstore business, "Scott's House of Books," which specializes in computer technology books. Creating an informational website for your own business is as simple as modifying this template.

Examining the Informational Website Template

An informational website serves as a form of online advertising for a business, just like flyers, newspaper ads, or catalogs do. Therefore, it makes sense to have the website template contain similar content.

Imagine that you needed to create a paper flyer for your company. What would this flyer contain? One thing you'd likely want to have displayed prominently is your company's name, address, and hours of business. Since the aim is to attract new customers, it's vital that you clearly provide information on how to get to the store! Additionally, you'd want the flyer to highlight the products or services your business focuses on selling. The flyer might also contain a list of the best-selling products, any specials or sales currently happening, or available coupons and discounts.

As this chapter's template shows (see Figure 6.1), an informational website contains similar information to a paper-based flyer. As you work with the template, keep in mind that the purpose of this website is to inform an existing or potential customer about your business, and to attract them to visit your store.

FIGURE 6.1

The informational website template.

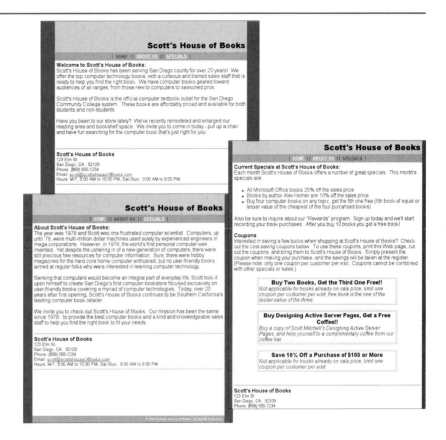

FIGURE 6.1

The informational website template.

As Figure 6.1 shows, the template contains three separate web pages. The home page provides a brief overview of Scott's House of Books. The About Us page gives a more in-depth look at the history of Scott's House of Books, while the Specials page lists current sales and cost-saving coupons. Notice that all of the pages provide a centered list of links near the top that provide quick links to the other pages in the website. Also, at the bottom of each page is information on the store's location, phone number, and hours of operation.

Customizing the Template

When creating an informational website, it is important to have the site's appearance reflect that of the business. This includes having the website use the same font and colors as the business's logo. This chapter's template's font and color scheme—the foreground and background colors used on each page—might differ radically from your company's logo. In the upcoming sections, you'll see how to tailor the template to meet your company's look.

"When creating an informational website, it is important to have the site's appearance reflect that of the business."

The template provided includes three pages: a home page, an About Us page, and a Specials page. You might need more or fewer pages for your company's information website. Adding or removing pages to the website requires that the navigational hyperlinks at the top of each page be updated accordingly, which we'll examine how to accomplish.

Changing the Web Page's Background Color

The content for each page in the website is included in the middle of each page on top of a white background. The background color of the areas left and right of the main content is a dark brown. If your company's logo has a dark brown background, this color scheme may be ideal. However, a company such as Coca-Cola, which is known for its red background, would insist that the background be changed from dark brown to the traditional Coca-Cola red.

Fortunately, changing this background color is a cinch. To customize the background color, perform the following steps:

1. Go to the Format menu

2. Choose the Page Colors and Backgrounds menu item. This will display the Page Colors and Backgrounds dialog box, which is shown in Figure 6.2.

3. ..ck on the brown button to the right of ..ckground label. This will display the

Block Background Color dialog box, which displays a palette of colors.

4. Once you have picked out a color from the palette, click the OK button to close the Block Background Color dialog box. The Page Colors and Backgrounds dialog box will show a preview of the background color you selected.

5. To confirm this selection, click the Page Colors and Backgrounds dialog box's OK button, which will return you to Composer with the web page's background changed to the color selected.

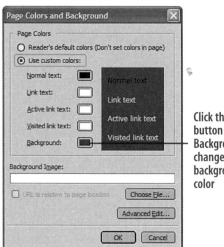

Click the brown button next to Background to change the background color

FIGURE 6.2

The Page Colors and Backgrounds dialog box allows you to customize the web page's colors.

Changing the Content Area Colors

The main content of each web page of the template is displayed using a black foreground on a white background. To tailor the template to better fit with your company's look, you might want to change these colors.

To change the foreground color of the text in the main content area, start by selecting the text whose color you want to change. (Recall that this can be done by clicking and holding down the mouse button as you drag the mouse cursor over the text you want to select.) Once you have selected the text, go to the Format menu and choose the Text Color menu option. This will display the Text Color dialog box (see Figure 6.3), from which you can choose the text's foreground color.

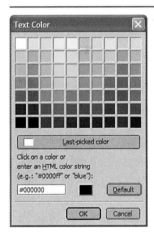

FIGURE 6.3

Pick the text's foreground color from the Text Color dialog box.

Changing the main content area's background color is a little more involved than setting its foreground color. The first step is to select the Table cell that contains the main content area's text. This can be accomplished in any of the following ways:

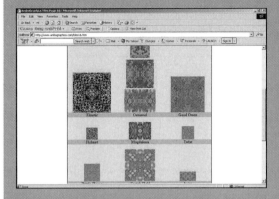

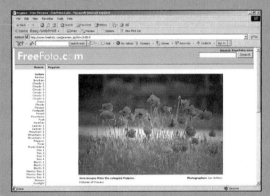

CAN'T BEAT FREE WEB GRAPHICS

Not artistic? Find free web graphics on the web to download for your own use. We found a site that categorizes free web graphics for you (http://www.freegraphics.com/). You can find buttons, bars, backgrounds, and clip art on many sites. Make sure to read the licensing information with each site. Sometimes the graphic images are only free if you're using them on a non-profit or personal basis. Here is a small list of cool sites we found:

Ambographics.com—offers lots of beautiful patterned backgrounds

Mikebonnell.com—has surreal-looking backgrounds and images

freefoto.com—where you can download stock quality photos for free

- ▶ By moving the mouse to the main content area, and clicking the left mouse button, while holding down the Ctrl key.

- ▶ By moving the mouse to the main content area, and clicking the right mouse button. This will bring up a context menu. From the Table Select menu item, choose the Cell option.

- ▶ By moving the mouse to the main content area and clicking once with the left mouse button. Following that, go to the Table menu, choose the Select menu item, and then pick the Cell option.

Once the Table cell has been selected, to change its background color go to the Table menu and choose the Table or Cell Background Color menu item. This will display the Table or Cell Color dialog box (which is virtually identical to the Text Color dialog box shown in Figure 6.3). Once you have selected a color and clicked OK, the main context area will show the chosen color.

> **NOTE**
>
> As always, when changing the background color of an area that contains text, make sure that the text color and selected background color have enough contrast to make the text easy to read.

Changing the Header's Background Color

Above the main content area in each page is a header that lists the company name (Scott's House of Books) in the bottom-right corner. Additionally, beneath the company name is a list of hyperlinks to the other pages of the website. As with the regions to the right and left of the main content area as well as the main content area itself, you might want to change the color scheme of the header to more closely align with your business's look or logo.

To change the background colors of either the company name or the navigational hyperlinks, you'll need to first select the region's Table cell and then pick the background color to use. Use the same steps discussed in the previous section, "Changing the Content Area Colors," to accomplish this.

You might also want to change the foreground color of either the company name or the navigational hyperlinks. For example, as you can see in the template pages in Figure 6.1, the current web page's hyperlink is a dark brown—the same color as the background outside of the main content area. The other two hyperlinks, however, are a bright white.

> **NOTE**
>
> The reason the current page's hyperlink is a dark brown is to give a visual cue to the viewer to help them ascertain what page they're currently viewing.

To change these colors, use the same steps discussed in the previous section. That is, select the text whose color you want to change, and then go to the Format menu and choose the Text Color menu option. See Table 6.1 for some quick tips on changing the color scheme.

TABLE 6.1	Quick Tips for Changing the Color Scheme
To Change the...	**Do the Following**
Page's background color	Go to the Format menu and choose the Page Colors and Backgrounds menu item, displaying the Page Colors and Backgrounds dialog box (see Figure 6.2). A palette of colors is displayed when you click the button to the right of the Background label. Choose the new color and click OK.
Content area text color	Select the text whose color you want to change and select the Text Color menu option from the Format menu. This will display the Text Color dialog box (see Figure 6.3). Pick the text color you want and click OK.
Content area background color	Move the mouse to the main content area and click the right mouse button. From the context menu, choose the Table Select menu item and pick the Cell option. Next, go to the Table menu and select the Table or Cell Background Color menu item, which will display a dialog box similar to the Text Color dialog box in Figure 6.3. Choose a color and click OK.
Header background color	Move the mouse to the header content area and click the right mouse button. From the context menu, choose the Table Select menu item and pick the Cell option. Next, go to the Table menu and select the Table or Cell Background Color menu item, which will display a palette of colors to choose one from.

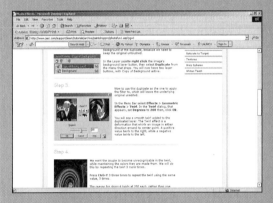

Adding or Removing Pages from the Template

The template provides three web pages for an informational website: a home page, an About

PAINT SHOP PRO

If you haven't heard about Paint Shop Pro yet, you should. This program that costs only $99 has almost as many features as Adobe Photoshop at a fraction of the price. It has effects packed into the program so that you can create halftones, 3D bubbles, different kinds of image distortions, tiled web page backgrounds and more. Their Community Gallery is especially cool. Users present some of their favorite projects that they completed in Paint Shop Pro. It's a great place to get ideas. And their Learning Center offers online tutorials for beginners. Download a trial version right from their website.

Us page, and a current Specials and Coupons page. When tailoring this template for your business you might want to forgo the About Us page, or perhaps your business has multiple locations, and you want a web page that lists all of these locations.

As we saw in Chapter 3, "Creating a Family/Personal Website," creating a new web page using the template can be done in one of two ways:

- ▶ By creating a new web page in Composer, and then copying and pasting the entire contents of a template page to the new page.
- ▶ By going to the File menu and choosing the Save As menu option, which has the effect of saving an existing template web page with a different filename.

Imagine that you used either of these two techniques to create an additional web page that listed all of your company's locations. How will a user find this page? Near the top of each page in the template there is a series of navigational hyperlinks (Home, About Us, and Specials). If you add a new page, you'll need to add a new hyperlink here. Similarly, if you remove a page from the template, you'll want to remove that page's hyperlink from this navigational section in the remaining pages.

Adding a New Navigational Hyperlink

When adding a new page to the website, you'll need to add some text to the navigational section of all of the pages in the site. Start by creating the web page that you want to add to the site, creating the content for this page. After you have finished creating the new page,

the next step is to add the text for this page in the navigation section.

Start by typing in the name of the newly added page in the navigation section. For example, if you just added a web page that listed all of your company's locations, you might use the name "Locations." In addition to typing in the page's name, you'll also want to include a separator. Notice that between each navigational hyperlink there is a vertical line (|), followed by a space, and followed by another vertical line. These characters serve as a separator between the text in the navigation section to make the navigation section easier to read. When typing in the text, be sure to first add this separator for consistency.

NOTE

On most keyboards you can type this character by holding down shift and pressing the backslash key (\). The backslash key is typically above the Enter key.

After typing the separator and text, all that remains is to specify the color for this text. The color to use for the text depends on what page you are editing. If you are following along, you should be working with the newly created page. The text you just added, then, is the name of the new page.

As Figure 6.1 showed, for each page in the website, the navigational section text color depends on the page itself. That is, the text for the current page is shown in a dark brown (the same color as the background color to the left and right of the main content area), while the text to other pages is white. The home page, for example, has the following text in its navigation link section: Home, About Us, and Specials. For the home page, the Home link is displayed in a dark brown, while the About Us and Special text is displayed in white.

> **NOTE**
>
> Using different colors for the text in the navigation section helps the visitor to the page determine what page they're currently viewing. Using visual cues such as color are useful in helping visitors quickly determine their location in the website.

Since you have just entered the text for the current page—such as "Location" for the page that lists store locations—choose the text color to be the same color as that of the region outside of the main content area. To choose the color for the text, first highlight the text and then go to the Format menu and select the Text Color menu option. (Refer back to the "Changing the Content Area Colors" section for a recap on setting text color.) You should select only the text, and not the vertical bar separator. That is, if you were entered the text ||Locations, you'd only want to change the color of Locations—leave the || as the default black color.

At this point, you have finished working on the newly added page. Save the page by going to the File menu and choosing the Save option. Next, you'll need to visit all of the other pages in the site and add the name for the newly created page.

For each of the other pages in the site, you'll next to complete the following steps:

1. Open the web page in Composer.

2. Add the name (along with the separator) of the newly created page in the page's navigational section. The name you type here should be the same you used earlier, such as "Location" for the page listing store locations.

3. Use the Format menu's Text Color option to make the added text white.

4. Convert the text into a hyperlink, directing the user to the appropriate page. Recall that to turn text into a hyperlink you first need to select the text, and then go to the Insert menu and choose the Link menu option. This will display the Link Properties dialog box (see Figure 6.4), from which you can choose the file to link to. (Naturally, you'll want to choose the file of the newly created web page.)

FIGURE 6.4

Specify a file from the Link Properties dialog box.

Be sure to complete these four steps for each of the web pages in the site. Figure 6.5 shows a screenshot of the home page after a link has been added to a fourth page.

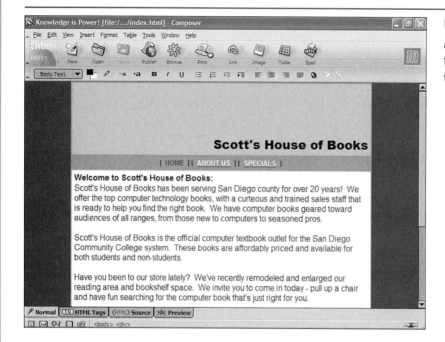

FIGURE 6.5
A link has been added from the home page to the Locations page.

CAUTION

When adding a link to the navigation section, be sure to follow the four steps provided in order. If you attempt to convert the text into a hyperlink before having it colored white, the text will become light blue, and you'll be unable to change the text color to white.

If you accidentally do convert the text into a hyperlink before changing its color to white, you'll need to revert the link back to plain text, make the text white, and then convert the text into a link. To revert the link back to text, right-click on the link and choose the Discontinue Link menu option.

Removing an Existing Navigational Hyperlink

The informational website template comes with three web pages. However, your business's site may only need one or two of these pages. If, for example, you decide your site does not need the About Us page, you'll want to take a moment to remove the link to the About Us page from the home page and Specials page.

To remove the link to a discontinued page, simply open all other web pages and delete the text (and vertical line separator) for the removed page. Again, be sure to do this for each web page in the site.

Customizing the Coupons

The Specials page in the informational website template provides cost-saving coupons and the current specials at Scott's House of Books (refer back to Figure 6.1 for a screenshot of the Specials page). The Specials page contains three coupons that the visitor can print out and redeem at the store's location. These coupons, though, are rather specific to Scott's House of Books. You'll likely want to add your own coupons, and perhaps have more than three available coupons.

> *"Editing a coupon's text is the same as editing any text in Composer. Just click inside the text, and start typing away!"*

Before delving into how to add new coupons and delete existing ones, first let's talk about how to edit the contents of an existing coupon. After all, if you want to offer three coupons for your company, there's no need to delete all three coupons provided in the template only to add three new ones yourself. Rather, you can simply edit the existing coupons to meet your needs.

Editing a coupon's text is the same as editing any text in Composer. Just click inside the text, and start typing away! You can use the text formatting options discussed in previous chapters to customize the look and feel of the coupon's text.

Adding a New Coupon

Adding a new coupon to the Specials page entails adding a table where you want the new coupon to appear. For example, if you want the coupon to appear beneath the other

coupons, place the mouse cursor beneath the last coupon and click to bring focus to that area. Once you have chosen the location for the new coupon, the next step is adding the table that will house the coupon's text.

To add a new table, go to the Table menu, choose the Insert submenu, and then pick the Table menu item. This will display the Insert Table dialog box. Opt to create a 1 row, 1 column table that's 75% of the width of the cell with a 1 pixel border. (Figure 6.6 shows a screenshot of the Insert Table dialog box after these settings have been made.)

> **NOTE**
>
> To add the new table inside of the main content area—which is, itself, a table—you must go to the Table menu, choose the Insert submenu, and select the Table menu item. That is, you *cannot* simply click the Table icon in the toolbar. Doing so would display the Table properties for the main content area table instead of adding a new table within the main content area table.

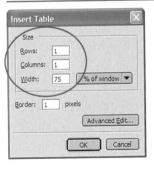

FIGURE 6.6

Add a one-column, one-row table with a 1 pixel border.

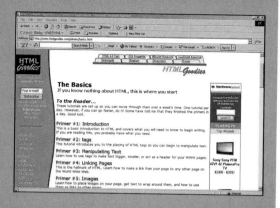

HTML GOODIES AND MORE!

You just can't have too many places to visit for good web-building tutorials. HTML Goodies, by Que author Joe Burns, offers primers for HTML, ad banners, JavaScript, Perl, CGI, ASP, database-SQL, XML, and much more. Joe assumes that you're a beginner and a non-programmer. For example, if you click on the ASP tutorial, he starts out by explaining what ASP is and why you might want to use it for your site. Then he gives you a short bit of code to type in and see if it works. You don't have to worry about understanding what the code means at first, but you can slowly learn the basics of ASP code as you follow the tutorial. What we liked about this site is that the information is not over-whelming to a beginner.

After clicking the OK button you will be returned to the Composer window and a one-column, one-row table will be inserted. At this point, this newly inserted table is left-aligned. Let's take a moment to center it. To center the table we need to edit the table's properties, so click inside this one-row, one-column table that was just created and then click the Table icon in the toolbar, or go to the Table menu and choose the Table Properties menu option. Doing so will display the Table Properties dialog box.

From the Table Properties dialog box choose the Table tab. From the Table tab you can configure the table's horizontal alignment by changing the drop-down list labeled "Table Alignment" from Left to Center. Figure 6.7 shows the Table Properties dialog box after this change has been made, and has circled the appropriate drop-down list that needs to be changed.

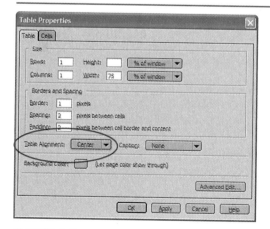

FIGURE 6.7

The table is centered via the "Table Alignment" drop-down list.

After setting the alignment of the table, click the OK button to return to the Composer window. At this point, the inserted table should be centered. All that remains is to add the text for the coupon. Click inside the table and start typing the terms of the coupon, such as: "Buy Two Books and Get a Third One Half Off the Sales Price!"

After you have entered the text for the first coupon, you can add additional coupons by repeating the steps outlined earlier. That is, add a new one-row, one-column table, center it, and enter the text for the coupon.

Removing an Existing Coupon

The template provides three coupons on the Specials page. Your business, however, might not want to display any coupons, or only one or two. In this case, you'll need to delete one or more of the coupons in the page. To accomplish this, start by clicking inside of the coupon that you want to delete. This will select the coupon's table.

Next, to delete the table go to the Table menu. From there, choose the Delete menu item, and then select the Table menu option. This will delete the table, thereby removing the coupon from the page.

> **NOTE**
> If you accidentally deleted the wrong coupon, don't worry! You can undo the delete by going to the Edit menu and choosing the Undo menu option.

Publishing the Website

To publish the site you'll need to publish each web page individually. Publish each web page by going to the File menu and choosing the Publish menu option. Since we've looked at publishing web pages to public websites extensively in previous chapters, we'll end our discussion here.

> **NOTE**
> For a more thorough description on publishing your website, refer back to the "Publishing Your Family/Personal Website" section in Chapter 3.

Summary

This chapter presented a template for informational websites, using a fictional bookstore company as the template example. An informational website provides current and prospective customers with information about the business including

- ▶ The business's location and hours
- ▶ The business's core products
- ▶ Current specials or sales
- ▶ Background information about the business, such as its history, mission statement, and so on

An informational website is another form of advertising, just like a newspaper ad or paper flyer. With the low cost of creating and hosting a public website, having an online presence is something any business can afford to do.

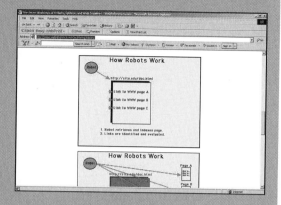

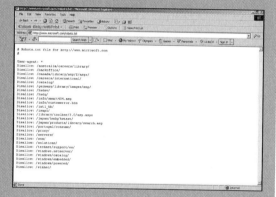

HOW SEARCH ENGINES FIND YOUR WEBSITE

Ever wonder how websites pop up in search engine results from Yahoo or Google? The article "The Inner Workings of Robots, Spiders, and Web Crawlers" by Lee Underwood explains how search engines find new websites and what you can do to help spiders and robots list your site properly. The article tells you how to create metatags that gives instructions to the robots and keywords for people looking for your type of site. Don't miss the bottom of the article, where the author gives you links to important robot validators, databases of Web robots, and places to stop spambots.

CHAPTER 6 CREATING AN INFORMATIONAL WEBSITE FOR YOUR BUSINESS

A business's informational website is its public, online face. Therefore, it's important that the website's design and colors match those of the business. In this chapter, you saw how to customize the template's color scheme, illustrating how easy customizing web pages is with Composer.

You also learned how to customize the coupons in the coupons page. Modifying the text of existing coupons is simple enough—just start typing away. You can also add new coupons or remove existing ones with just a few clicks of the mouse.

While informational websites are a great means to inform customers of your products and their prices, they still require the user to make a trek to the store to actually make a purchase. As the Internet's popularity has grown, a number of businesses have sprung up that sell their products via the Internet. This trend will continue its explosive pace as more businesses start selling online and as more people feel comfortable making purchases over the Internet. In the next and final chapter, "Creating an Online Store Front," we'll look at creating a website from which customers can directly buy products!

CHAPTER 7

Creating an Online Storefront

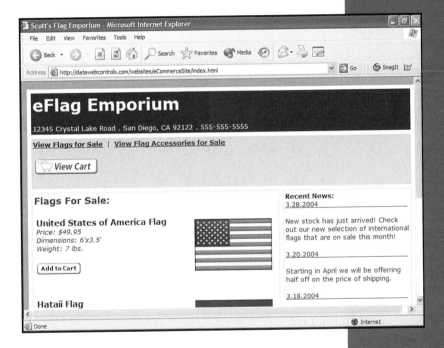

In the previous chapter, "Creating an Informational Website for Your Business," you looked at a template for a website designed to provide information about a company's products. As discussed, many consumers today are utilizing the Internet to do research on products before they buy them, in order to find out the various options available and price compare among competing local retailers. The informational website, however, is limited in that it only provides information about the products and services available—it does not provide a means for directly purchasing the products.

> "As the popularity of the Internet has ballooned over the years, many businesses have begun making their inventory available for purchase online. These types of websites marry commerce and the Internet, and are hence referred to as eCommerce websites."

As the popularity of the Internet has ballooned over the years, many businesses have begun making their inventory available for purchase online. These types of websites marry commerce and the Internet, and are hence referred to as eCommerce websites. There is a plethora of eCommerce websites selling a wide range of products online. Amazon.com, one of the most well-known eCommerce sites, sells a vast array of products, from books to video games and DVDs to kitchenware and garden tools.

Successful eCommerce websites have been built for both companies choosing to sell strictly online, and those companies who have had decades of history selling products in traditional brick and mortar stores. For example, Amazon.com is one of many companies that sell products exclusively on the Internet. That is, there are not any Amazon.com stores where you can stroll into and peruse the inventory. Wal-Mart, the world's largest brick and mortar retailer with close to 5,000 stores worldwide, also has an eCommerce site—http://www.WalMart.com.

An eCommerce website must provide the following functionality:

- Display the items for sale along with their prices.
- Provide a means for a user to add one or more items to their "shopping cart."
- Accept payment information from a customer. (This typically involves the customer providing their credit card number.)

In this chapter, you will build your very own eCommerce website that implements these features.

Accepting credit card payments and maintaining a shopping cart are anything but trivial tasks. Fortunately, PayPal provides a Merchant Account program that provides a means for processing credit card payments and for supporting a shopping cart interface. There are no upfront costs associated with using the PayPal Merchant Account—the only cost is a small percentage of the total sales. The "Creating a PayPal Merchant Account" section discusses these fees and how to get started creating a PayPal Merchant Account.

NOTE

The three requirements for an eCommerce site—listing the items for sale, providing a shopping cart, and accepting payment—are the minimum needed. Many eCommerce websites offer additional functionality, such as searching the products for sale, sorting the products by price or name, and allowing users to leave feedback about various products.

The eCommerce site we'll be creating this chapter will not include any of these more advanced features. The site will, however, be fully functional, allowing visitors to buy products directly from our website.

Examining the eCommerce Website Template

All eCommerce websites provide a core set of functionality. Since the purpose of an eCommerce website is to provide a means for a visitor to purchase products online, the eCommerce site must list the products for sale, allow the user to add one or more products to his shopping cart, and finally provide a means for the user to purchase the products.

The eCommerce site template is one for a fictional company—eFlags Direct—that sells flags online. eFlags Direct sells both flags and flag accessories, such as flag poles, ropes, clips, and so on. The eFlags Direct template breaks up its products for sale into two categories: Flags and Flag Accessories. From the Flags category, users can add one or more flags to their shopping cart.

WHAT IS AN ONLINE SHOPPING CART?

If you've ever purchased something online, you likely are familiar with online shopping carts. For those who have not yet purchased something online, though, an online shopping cart is similar in concept to a grocery store shopping cart—it simply serves as a receptacle into which you can place your items prior to purchasing.

The user experience of an online shopping cart goes as follows: a visitor browses through the eCommerce website, checking out the products for sale. If she finds a particular item she'd like to purchase, she clicks the Add Item to Cart button next to the item of interest. This adds the item to the shopping cart. At this point, the shopper can continue to browse through the items for sale, adding additional items to the shopping cart.

Once our shopper has finished browsing and is ready to check out, she can click a Checkout button that will present her with a bill and ask for payment information. At this time our shopper would enter her credit card information.

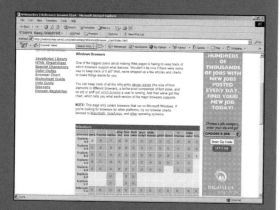

DOES YOUR WEBSITE LOOK RIGHT IN EVERY BROWSER?

Webmonkey is a particularly good site for tutorials on web building. We found a nice article and chart on what standards different browsers support. You may design and test your website using the browser on your computer. It may look fine to you, but what about all of your visitors and the browsers they're using? If you check out the browser statistics on www.counter.com, you'll find that 77% of people are using Microsoft Internet Explorer 6.x and 16% are using Internet Explorer 5.x. That at least narrows it down for you when you're trying to make sure your site can be viewed properly by most people. If you want to accommodate more people than that, pay attention to the standards on Mozilla, Netscape, Safari, and Opera, too.

In addition to listing the products for sale, shoppers must be able to add products to their shopping cart. Creating a shopping cart is not a trivial task, and requires advanced computer programming skills that are far beyond the scope of this book. Fortunately, PayPal offers a shopping cart that can be plugged into the eCommerce website template by inserting a few lines of HTML.

The last vital piece of an eCommerce website is accepting payment, which involves showing the user their balance due. The amount they owe is typically the sum of the products purchased, any sales tax that needs to be added, plus any shipping costs. After reviewing their shopping cart and balance due, the user is prompted to enter their credit card information and complete the transaction.

As with the shopping cart, creating a web page to provide a bill, to accept payment information, and to properly bill it, is far beyond the scope of this book. As with the shopping cart, PayPal provides a means for payment that can be plugged into our eCommerce website.

The eCommerce website template is shown in Figure 7.1. Notice that it's composed of two pages: a list of the flags for sale and a list of the flag accessories for sale. Each item for sale includes a picture, a description, and an Add to Cart button. Clicking the Add to Cart button adds the item to the user's PayPal shopping cart. A user can check out by clicking the View Cart hyperlink.

FIGURE 7.1

The eCommerce website template.

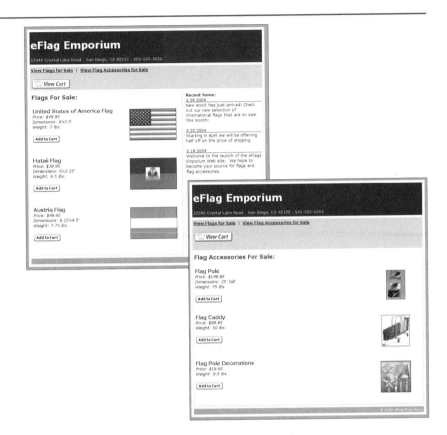

FIGURE 7.1

The eCommerce website template.

Working with the eCommerce website template will require a little more customization than required with previous templates. First, you will have to create a free Merchant Account through PayPal.com. Then, based on your merchant information, you will need to tailor the Add to Cart button and View Cart hyperlink.

Customizing the Home Page

The eCommerce website template's home page starts by listing the company's name, address, and contact information at the top of the page. Underneath that, there are a series of navigational hyperlinks listing the product categories, along with a View Cart button.

To change the name of one of the product categories, click on the product category text and, using the keyboard, alter the link's text. To change the URL to which the hyperlink points to, right-click on the link and choose the Link Properties menu option. This, as you've seen in previous chapters, will display the Link Properties dialog box, from which you can change the link's location.

> **TIP**
>
> To create a new navigational link, set the focus to the point where you want the new link to be placed. Then, go to the Insert menu and choose the Link menu option. This will display the Link Properties dialog box, prompting you for the link's text and location.

The View Cart button links to PayPal.com's website and, when clicked, displays the items in the user's shopping cart and provides a checkout process. You'll need to configure this View Cart button based on your own PayPal.com Merchant Account. The next section examines the steps necessary to create a Merchant Account and to configure the View Cart button.

Underneath the navigation hyperlinks are two table cells. The one on the left lists the flags for sale. The one on the right lists recent site news.

The template contains descriptions and pictures for flags. If you're selling something other than flags, you'll of course need to change the description and pictures. To edit the picture, right-click on the picture and choose the Image Properties menu option. This will display the Image Properties dialog box from

which you can specify the image file to use, along with its dimensions and other aesthetic properties.

At the end of each product description there's an Add to Cart button. This button ties into PayPal.com to integrate a shopping cart with the eCommerce site. To have this button work correctly, you'll need to first create a PayPal.com Merchant Account.

Configuring the Add to Cart Buttons

The next challenge is to allow visitors to add items from the View Flags for Sale and View Flag Accessories for Sale web pages to their shopping cart. In order to accomplish this, you can use PayPal's Merchant Account tools, which include capabilities to add a shopping cart to a website, as well as a means for processing credit card payments.

To allow visitors to add a flag or flag accessory to their shopping cart, add a button titled Add to Cart for each item for sale. By clicking this button, the specified item will be added to the user's shopping cart. The shopper may then add additional items to their shopping cart and eventually pay for their purchased items.

Before you can examine what needs to be done to provide the Add to Cart button for each product, you first need to register for a PayPal Merchant Account. There are no costs or fees associated with creating a PayPal Merchant Account, so feel free to follow along in creating your own Merchant Account!

Creating a PayPal Merchant Account

PayPal—on the Web at http://www.paypal.com— was founded in 1998 to allow individuals and businesses to send and receive payments easily, reliably, and securely. Anyone can create a free PayPal account, and then transfer money into their account by sending PayPal a check, by having the money drafted from their bank, or through a credit card transaction. Once the money is in your account, you can send the money to another PayPal member by simply supplying that person's email address and the amount you want to send. You can, at any time, withdraw all or part of the funds in your PayPal account, either through a direct deposit into your bank account or via a check.

NOTE

In 2002, PayPal was acquired by eBay. Not surprisingly, eBay strongly encourages using PayPal as a means for paying for auctions on eBay.

Since its inception, PayPal has continued to offer more features to facilitate its main goal of allowing online payments. One added feature is the PayPal Merchant Account, which is designed to allow individuals and small businesses to accept payments online. The Merchant Account provides a shopping cart and a payment process, both of which reside on PayPal's website.

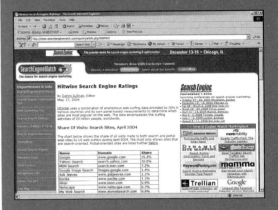

HOW DO PEOPLE FIND YOUR SITE?

In a previous sidebar, we mentioned web robots and crawlers that search engines use to detect sites on the Internet. If you want to know which search engines are most popular, go to Search Engine Watch, and you'll discover where most people go to find sites. The majority of searchers, 15%, go to Google.com to look for websites. If you want to get noticed or advertise to your customers, the majority of your time and resources should go into making sure that Google knows your site and lists it properly. On the other hand, more people visit the Yahoo.com portal every day—29%. It's a good home page for any browser because it offers up-to-date news, a link to email, stock reports, and other useful links. Find out from Search Engine Watch how to submit your site to these portals and optimize your listing.

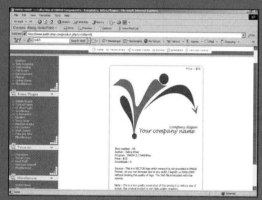

ANIMATE YOUR SITE

What if you want animations for your site, but you're not a Macromedia Flash designer? Check out Flash Components and buy animations that you can customize for your site. The components require you to have Flash on your computer, so it still may not be an inexpensive proposition. If you want a cheaper alternative, download the program Swish, which creates animations as well. Most of the components and templates on www.swish-shop.com were $50 and under. To download Swish, visit swishzone.com. For $15, you can even buy a vector-based logo design for your company or your site.

The Merchant Account works as follows:

1. A user visits your site and finds a product they are interested in buying.

2. The shopper clicks the Add to Cart button next to the desired product's name, which takes them to PayPal's website, adds the item to the shopping cart, and displays the shopping cart. The user can, at that point, check out by paying for the item, or can return to your website to continue shopping.

3. When the customer has completed their shopping, they return to the shopping cart on PayPal's website and enter their payment information. After successfully providing their payment information, they are sent back to your website.

If a customer makes a purchase from your website of, say, $10.00, what happens is the following: PayPal charges the user's credit card for $10.00. After the monies have been cleared, PayPal takes a small percentage of the sale—2.2% plus a 30 cent transaction fee. The remainder of the balance is then credited into your PayPal account. Also, after a payment has been processed, you are sent an email informing you of the purchase so that you can ship the shopper's goods to her.

Figure 7.2 provides an illustration of the process of a visitor making a purchase from your website. What's important to realize is that the shopping cart and payment processing are done entirely on PayPal's website. This has several advantages, the big ones being that you can sell products on your site without needing to process credit card transactions or concern yourself with the complexities involved in setting up an online shopping cart and payment processing.

FIGURE 7.2

PayPal handles the shopping cart and payment processing on their website.

STEP 1

A shopper finds a product he likes on your Web site and clicks the "Add to Cart" button.

STEP 2

The user is whisked to PayPal's Web site, where they see their shopping cart.

STEP 3

The shopper returns to your Web site and adds additional items to his shopping cart...

STEP 4

The user completes his shopping and returns to PayPal's site to "checkout." The user enters his credit card information, completing the transaction.

STEP 5

PayPal takes a small percentage off the top of the total transaction value, and sends the remainder of the purchase price to your PayPal account

PayPal offers accounts for both individuals and businesses. Business accounts have access to the Merchant Account features by default. Personal accounts are broken into two classes:

- ▶ Basic Accounts
- ▶ Premier Accounts

Basic Accounts do not impose any sort of fee on receiving or sending money, but do not offer the features available with the Merchant Account. Upgrading to a Premier account grants you access to the Merchant Account tools, but beware—*all* payments—not just credit card payments—will be subject to a 2.2%–2.9% fee off the top.

FIGURE 7.3

The Account Overview screen informs existing PayPal members what type of account they have.

If you have an existing PayPal basic personal account, the first step is to determine what type of account you have. To do this, log in to your PayPal account. In the Account Overview screen you will see what type of account you have. As Figure 7.3 shows, I have a U.S. Personal Account.

If you do not have a Premier account, you will need to upgrade your account. In the Account Overview screen you should find a link titled Upgrade Account. Click this to begin the upgrade process.

If you do not have a PayPal account at all, you will need to create a new Premier account. This process is free, and only takes a few moments of your time. Start by going to PayPal's home page—http://www.paypal.com—and click on one of the Sign Up links shown in Figure 7.4.

You will first be asked whether you want to create a Personal or Business account, and for which country (see Figure 7.5). If you choose a Personal account you will be asked for information such as your name, address, phone number, email address, and so on. If you create a business account, you will need to provide this information as well as information about the business, such as what field it's in, your role in the business, the business's official contact information, and so on.

FIGURE 7.4

Click on one of the Sign Up links to create a new PayPal account.

FIGURE 7.5

Choose to create a business or personal account.

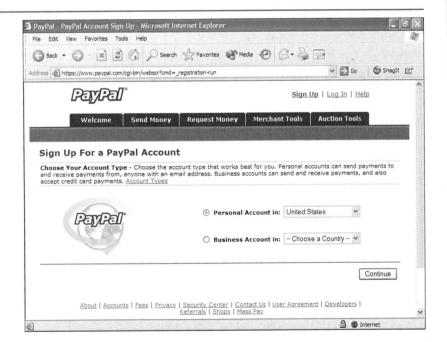

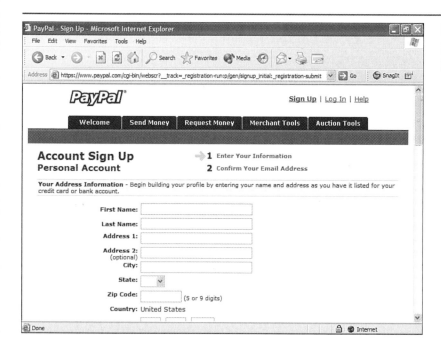

FIGURE 7.6

Provide your personal information.

If you opted to create a business account, you will be prompted for information about the business. After entering this information, you will be asked to provide the personal information shown in Figure 7.6. (If you created a personal account you will be taken directly to the screen shown in Figure 7.6.) Here you are asked to provide your name, address, phone number, email address, a password, and other information. For personal accounts, you can choose whether you want to create this account as a Premier account—choose Yes.

The final step involves sending a confirmation email to the email address you supplied. Follow the instructions in the email you receive to complete the registration process.

Congratulations! At this point, you have created a PayPal account that has access to the Merchant Account features.

Getting the Add to Cart Button HTML

In order to allow your visitors to add an item to their shopping cart, you need to add an Add to Cart button next to each product for sale on your website. The button, when clicked, will direct the user to PayPal's website, adding the item to the user's shopping cart.

NOTE

In the template, there already is an Add to Cart button. To customize the template for your site, you'll need to delete this button and add in your customized button.

> *"PayPal offers a wizard that steps you through the process of adding an Add to Cart button."*

In previous chapters, you saw how hyperlinks can be used to transfer a user from one web page to another. In addition to hyperlinks, there are also more involved techniques for transferring a user from one page to another. One such technique involves the use of *forms*. A thorough discussion of forms is beyond the scope of this book—it is mentioned solely because this is the technique used to transfer the user from our website to PayPal's website when adding an item to the shopping cart or when checking out.

Don't worry; you don't have to be a wiz at forms to create the Add to Cart buttons. Rather, PayPal offers a wizard that steps you through the process of adding an Add to Cart button. At the end of the wizard, you are given a snippet of HTML markup, which can be directly pasted into our web page where we want the Add to Cart button to appear.

WEBSITE REVIEW

http://www.internic.net/whois.html

I'M READY FOR MY OWN DOMAIN NAME

If you're starting a business online or you want to own a domain name, you'll need to know which ones are already taken. InterNIC runs a page called WhoIs, where you can type in a domain that you want to own and find out if it's in use or for sale. As an example, let's say that we might want to create a domain for this book. If you type in "createwebsite.com" into the WhoIs search window, you'll find that Tucows Inc. owns that particular domain name. They bought it in August 2001, and the name expires in August 2006. Happy searching.

The first step to generating the Add to Cart button HTML is to go to PayPal's website and log in. Next, click on the Merchant Tools tab at the top of any PayPal web page. This will take you to the Merchant Account home page, shown in Figure 7.7. From the Merchant Account home page, click the Paypal Shopping Cart hyperlink.

This will begin a two-page process where you will be asked a number of questions about the product being sold, such as its title, price, item number, and other information. Let's create the button HTML for the United States of America flag. The first page of the two-page wizard starts by asking you to supply the Item Name, Item ID, Price of Item, and Currency.

TIP

The Item ID field is optional, but is useful if you are selling a large number of items. When a user makes a purchase from your site, you'll receive an email with a list of what products she bought. This will include the product name, along with the Item ID (if provided). So, if you keep track of your products by some ID, enter this ID into the Item ID field.

Figure 7.8 shows a screenshot of the first page of the wizard after suitable values have been entered into these fields for the United States flag. (Note that I arbitrarily chose 311 as the Item ID for the U.S. flag.)

FIGURE 7.8

The first step involves providing information about the product for sale.

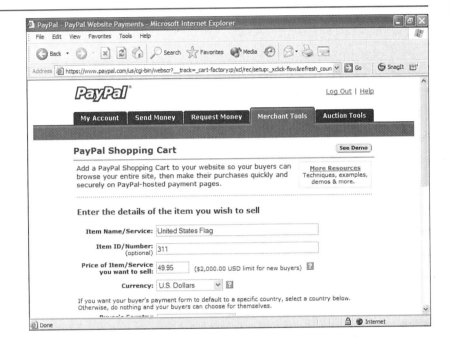

After you have entered the product's name, ID, price, and so on, scroll down to the bottom of this first page. You'll be prompted to select an Add to Cart button. PayPal provides a default button (shown in Figure 7.9), but if you have a custom-made button you can supply the URL of this button image. I am going to opt to stick with the PayPal-provided image.

If you do not need to add any additional features, such as sales tax or shipping costs, you can click the Create Button Now button. Otherwise, if you want to specify more advanced features, click the Add More Options button.

NOTE

If you clicked the Create Button Now because you did not need to specify shipping costs or sales tax information, feel free to skip over the "Specifying Sales Tax and Shipping Costs" section and go directly to the "Viewing the Button's HTML" section.

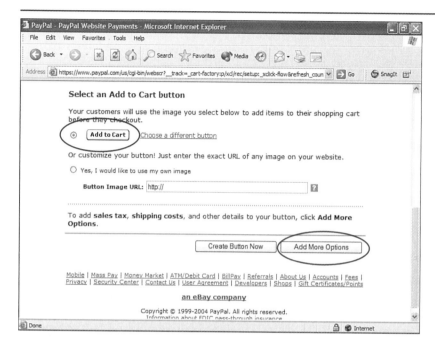

FIGURE 7.9

Click the Add More Options button to provide information on sales tax and shipping costs.

Specifying Sales Tax and Shipping Costs

If you click the Add More Options button from the first page of the wizard, you will be taken to the second page, where you can, among other things, specify sales tax and shipping costs. Figure 7.10 shows the Shipping and Sales Tax section on the second page. Note that by default there is no shipping costs or sales tax applied.

To provide a shipping cost, click the Edit button to the right of the shipping cost list. There are two types of shipping cost models that you can choose from:

► Flat—Here, the shipping cost is a flat cost based on price ranges. That is, you can opt to have all items between $0.00 and $9.99 cost, say, $2.50 to ship, while other items between $10.00 and $49.99 might cost $4.95 to ship.

► Percentage—Here, the shipping cost is a percentage of the total cost. You can enter different percentages for different price ranges. That is, you can have items between $0.00 and $100.00 require a shipping cost of 10% of the purchase price, while items above $100.00 could have a shipping cost of 7.5%.

FIGURE 7.10

You can specify the shipping costs and sales tax.

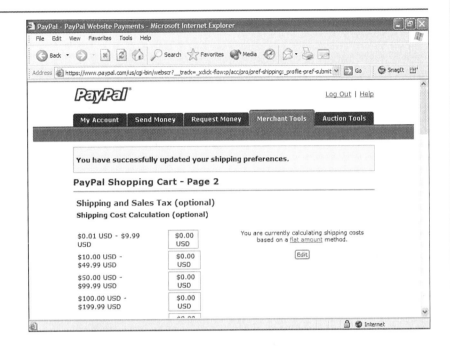

To edit the sales tax, click the Edit button to the right of the Sales Tax Calculation section. The sales tax section lets you add certain taxes for shoppers from particular countries or U.S. states. For example, if your business is based in California, only California residents who purchase goods through your website need pay sales tax. PayPal allows you to specify what countries or states must pay sales tax and what the tax rate is for each state or country.

When checking out, the customer's bill totals the sum of the prices of items purchased, plus the shipping costs, if specified, plus any sales tax, if specified and if applicable based on the buyer's residence.

There are some additional options on this web page, but these are a bit beyond the scope of this book. After providing the shipping and sales tax information, scroll down to the bottom of the page and click the Create Button Now button to view the button's generated HTML markup.

NOTE

You only need to set up the shipping costs and sales tax once. After specifying this information, it is stored on PayPal's web servers so that for all products you sell the sales tax and shipping cost information is applied.

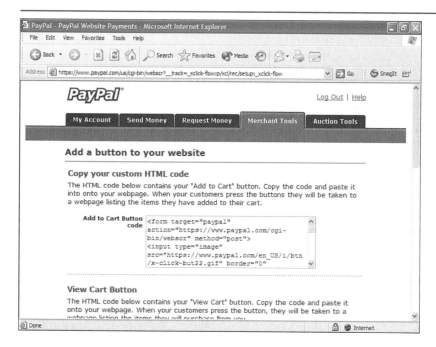

FIGURE 7.11

The HTML markup for the button has been generated.

Viewing the Button's HTML

After you have clicked the Create Button Now button—either in the first page of the wizard or after entering shipping and sales tax information—you will be taken to the final page that contains the HTML markup for the Add to Cart buttons. Figure 7.11 shows a screenshot of this page.

There are actually two snippets of HTML on this page. The first one is in the textbox labeled "Add to Cart Button code." This HTML markup is what you will place next to the United States Flag product. Doing so will display an Add to Cart button. The second snippet of HTML is in the text box labeled "View Cart Button code."

The HTML in this second text box will be used to take the user to his shopping cart. Specifically, it will display a button titled View Cart. In the "Viewing the Shopping Cart" section you'll see how to add this View Cart button.

TIP

At the bottom of this page you'll find a button titled Create Another Button. Clicking this button will take you back to the first page of the wizard with your previous values pre-entered into the various text boxes. You'll need to create an Add to Cart button for each product for sale on our site. The Create Another Button button is a quick way to jump back and start creating a new button!

Adding the Add to Cart Button into the Template

To customize the template's Add to Cart button with your own PayPal.com merchant information, you'll need to first delete the existing Add to Cart button. Notice that around the button is a green, dashed border. To remove the Add to Cart button, right-click on this border and choose the Delete menu option.

NOTE

After deleting the Add to Cart button, the green, dashed border should disappear. If you still see the green, dashed border, but without the button, try again, making sure to right-click on the dashed border.

Once you have deleted the Add to Cart button in the template, you're ready to add your custom Add to Cart button. To accomplish this you'll need to copy and paste the HTML from the PayPal.com wizard's "Add to Cart Button code" text box to the appropriate location in the web page.

First go to the PayPal web page and copy the HTML in the first text box to your computer's clipboard. (This is accomplished by first selecting the text in text box and then going to the Edit menu and choosing Copy.)

Now, return to the Composer window. To insert the HTML copied from the PayPal web page, go to the Insert menu and choose the HTML menu option. This will display the Insert HTML dialog box (shown in Figure 7.12). Paste the HTML from your computer's clipboard into this

dialog box by hitting the Control (Ctrl) and V keys on your keyboard simultaneously.

FIGURE 7.12

The Insert HTML dialog box allows you to add HTML markup to a specific section of the web page.

After you have pasted in the HTML from the PayPal web page, click the Insert button to paste this HTML content into the web page.

Congratulations, you have added your first Add to Cart button! Now, this process needs to be repeated for each of the other products for sale. That is, you'll need to return to the PayPal website and repeat the wizard, entering in a different product's title, price, and other pertinent information. Do this for both the flag and flag accessories for sale.

NOTE

Realize that you only need to supply shipping costs and sales tax *once*. That is, you do not need to repeatedly provide this information for each button created.

Viewing the Shopping Cart

The final step in creating the eCommerce site is to add a View Cart button to the navigational bar at the top of each web page in the site template. Recall that when generating the HTML markup for an individual Add to Cart button in the PayPal.com wizard, there were two text boxes of HTML—the first one contained the HTML markup for the Add to Cart button, while the second text box contained the HTML markup for the View Shopping Cart button. (Refer back to Figure 7.11 for a screenshot.) You need to paste the HTML from the second text box where you want the View Shopping Cart button to appear.

> *"The final step in creating the eCommerce site is to add a View Cart button to the navigational bar at the top of each web page in the site template."*

Like with the Add to Cart button, to accomplish this you'll first need to delete the View Cart button from each template page. Following that, you'll need to paste in the HTML from the wizard using the Insert menu's HTML option.

Once you have added your customized View Cart button, users will be able to view their cart's contents at any time by clicking on the View Cart button.

Tying It All Together—A True Online Shopping Experience

At this point, you have created the essential pieces of an eCommerce site: you have listed the products for sale; each product has an Add to Cart button next to it, which adds it to the shopping cart; and customers can provide their credit card information and purchase the goods in their shopping cart. Your task was made infinitely easier thanks to the Merchant Account tools provided by PayPal.

You're now ready to go live with your site! As discussed in the four previous chapters, this involves publishing each page. Take a moment to open each template's two web pages and publish them by clicking the Publish icon in the toolbar, or by going to File menu and selecting the Publish menu item.

Now that you've published your site, let's take a moment to look at the shopper's experience—from browsing the products, to adding items to the shopping cart, to paying for an order.

Figure 7.13 shows the "View Flags for Sale" web page. Note that each flag for sale has an Add to Cart button. If a visitor clicks, say, the Austrian Flag Add to Cart button, a new browser window opens showing the user their shopping cart (see Figure 7.14).

FIGURE 7.13

A shopper would first visit the "View Flags for Sale" web page.

FIGURE 7.14

Clicking the Add to Cart button takes the user to their shopping cart.

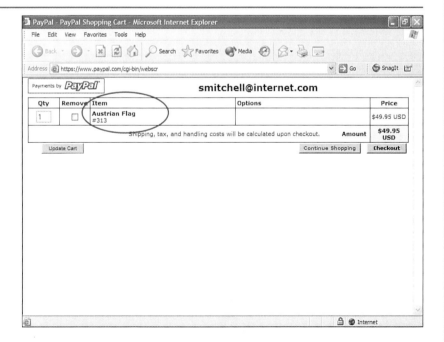

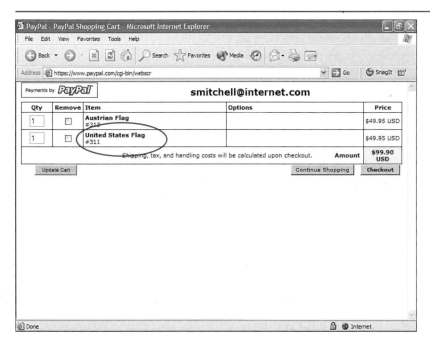

FIGURE 7.15

The user has added the United States Flag to her shopping cart.

As Figure 7.14 shows, the shopping cart lists the current items the user has added to their cart. From this page the user can update the quantity of items in their cart or remove items. By clicking the Continue Shopping button, the user will be returned to the "View Flags for Sale" web page, where they can add additional flags to their shopping cart. Figure 7.15 shows the shopping cart after the user returns to the "View Flags for Sale" web page and clicks the Add to Cart button for the United States Flag.

The user completes her purchase by clicking the Checkout button in the shopping cart. Doing so takes the shopper to a page that spells out the payment details and offers the user the opportunity to pay through an existing PayPal account (if they have one), or via a credit card. Figure 7.16 shows the first screen of the Payment Details page.

After progressing through the payment screens, which involve either logging in to an existing PayPal account or providing credit card information, the user is billed and your PayPal account is credited with the amount of the transaction less the percentage PayPal takes off the top.

After the transaction has completed, you will receive an email indicating what items the user has purchased and their shipping address. It is then your responsibility to send them their purchased goods in a timely manner.

FIGURE 7.16

The user can pay for her purchase via an existing PayPal account or with a credit card.

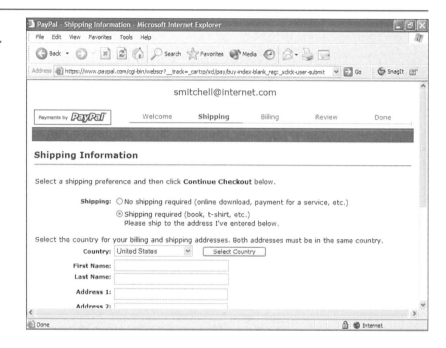

Summary

In this chapter, you learned how to create a fully functioning online store with the aid of PayPal's Merchant Account tools. All the complicated work of creating and maintaining a shopping cart, and processing credit card payments, is handled by PayPal for a small commission on sales.

The eCommerce site we built was a relatively simple one, containing just the bare features required: a listing of the products; an Add to Cart button for each product that, when clicked, added the item to the shopping cart;

and a means for customers to check out and pay for their order. More advanced eCommerce sites typically contain additional features, such as customization features, search capabilities, and customer feedback. Unfortunately, adding these sorts of features would require more advanced technologies than HTML, and therefore fall outside the scope of this book. Don't let the simplicity of the eCommerce website we created, though, take away from what we accomplished. In the span of one chapter we went from nothing to a website that provides a fully functioning online store front.

CONCLUSION

Congratulations on Your Progress!

Over the past several chapters, we looked at creating five separate websites:

▶ A family website, where we could share the latest news and photos of our family with distant friends and relatives.

▶ A hobby website, sharing the rules, tips, and tricks of the game of chess with others who share the same interest.

▶ A website for an organization, specifically for a fictional botanical club. The organizational website served as an information portal for both current participants and potential members.

▶ An informational website for a fictional book store that listed the store's current sales, cost-saving coupons, and important information, like the store's address, phone number, and hours of operation.

▶ An eCommerce website for a fictional flag company. The eCommerce site highlighted PayPal's Merchant Account tools, which allow ordinary websites to provide a shopping cart and accept credit card payments.

If you followed along at your computer, you not only saw how these sites were quickly and easily constructed using Composer, but you also built them yourself from the ground up. Congratulations! The driving purpose of this book was to show you just how easy and fun it can be to create websites. Hopefully, you found this journey to be both entertaining and rewarding!

You may be wondering, "What next?" What's the next step for someone who wants to continue learning about website development and design? There are a number of books and websites I'd recommend as next steps for those interested in continuing along this path.

Learning HTML

Since we used Composer, a WYSIWYG tool, for building the five websites, we didn't examine HTML at all. Remember that web pages are composed of HTML syntax, which is a special language for specifying the structure of a web page. With Composer, the HTML was written for us automatically.

While you can definitely continue in website development without a thorough background in HTML, I find it helps to be familiar with HTML. Also, some readers might be interested in learning more about what happens behind the scenes of Composer, and are interested in studying the real language behind web pages. For those folks ready to jump into HTML, I highly recommend *Sams Teach Yourself HTML 4.0 in 24 Hours*, by Dick Oliver (ISBN 0-672-31724-9).

There are also numerous websites that provide tutorials, articles, and lessons for learning the specifics of HTML. One site I personally use all the time is W3Schools.com. They have a great set of interactive lessons worth checking out. You can see their HTML information at http://www.w3schools.com/html/.

Upgrading from Composer

The saying, "You get what you pay for" holds true for many things in life, including web page editing software. Composer is a good enough tool for creating basic websites, and is a great product to learn with since it's both intuitive to use and doesn't cost a dime. However, there are more professional-grade web page editors that, while more expensive, have many more features and tools to aid in creating more impressive websites.

One of the most popular website editing tools is Macromedia DreamWeaver (http://www.macromedia.com/software/dreamweaver/). DreamWeaver offers a WYSIWYG tool, like Composer, but with more options and features. Another common tool is Microsoft FrontPage (http://www.microsoft.com/frontpage/).

DreamWeaver and FrontPage's features come at a cost, unfortunately. At the time of this writing, DreamWeaver costs $399.00, while FrontPage runs $199.00. If you are serious about website design, though, these tools are well worth their cost.

Thank You for Reading!

Before I leave, let me thank you for reading my book! I hope you enjoyed our time together and not only learned how easy it is to create web pages, but also had a fun time as well. If you have any comments or suggestions on the book or its content, please do not hesitate to contact me at mitchell@4guysfromrolla.com.

Thanks!

—*Scott Mitchell*

mitchell@4guysfromrolla.com

BONUS CHAPTER

When writing this book I wanted to focus on the task at hand: showing how to easily create your own websites by customizing provided templates using Mozilla Composer. There were some peripheral topics that I wanted to include, but felt that their inclusion into the book's text detracted from its main purpose. Instead, these tangents are instead presented here, as a Bonus Chapter.

The Bonus Chapter contains three sections:

▶ **HTML—The Language of Web Pages—** While Composer makes creating and editing web pages as simple as editing or creating a document with a word processor, underneath the covers Composer is generating appropriate *HTML*. HTML is the markup language used to create web pages. This section, which was initially in Chapter 2, "Creating a Website," provides a discussion on what HTML is and its purpose.

▶ **Understanding How the Internet Works—** To visit a website, all you have to do is enter the site's name into your browser's Address window. But how does your computer, based on a website name alone, know how to get the specified web page from the appropriate web server? This section, which was initially in Chapter 2, examines how Internet-connected computers are addressed and how special computers called *DNS servers* act as a phone book on the Internet, tying domain names to web server addresses.

▶ **Optimizing Your Digital Pictures—** Many digital cameras take high-resolution photographs that are oftentimes far too large in both dimensions and file size. After taking images from a digital camera, you'll likely want to resize the images to a smaller dimension. This section discusses some important digital picture terminology and shows how to resize those large image files.

As with the book, if you have any comments or questions regarding the Bonus Chapter, please don't hesitate to drop me an email at mitchell@4guysfromrolla.com.

HTML—The Language of Web Pages

Whenever you navigate to a web page through a web browser, the browser requests the page from the appropriate web server and displays the retrieved page. Recall that the web page itself is nothing more than a file on the web server. The file's contents describe how the page should be displayed in the browser.

"A web page defines how it is to be displayed using a markup language called Hypertext Markup Language, or HTML."

Specifically, a web page defines how it is to be displayed using a markup language called *Hypertext Markup Language*, or *HTML*. HTML defines how content should be displayed in a web page. It uses *tags* to indicate formatting. For example, the *bold tag*, denoted `<b>`, indicates that its inner text should be displayed in a bold font. The *italic tag*, `<i>`, indicates that its inner text should be displayed in italics. Given the following HTML markup in a web page, Figure B.1 shows what would be displayed in a web browser.

```
This is <b>bold</b> while this is
<i>italic</i>.
This, you'll see, is both <b><i>bold
and italic</i></b>.
```

FIGURE B.1

HTML specifies how content should be formatted.

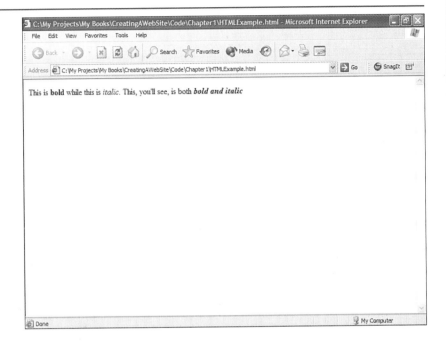

The important thing to realize is that every web page you visit with your browser is composed of HTML markup. It is this markup that describes how to display the web page in your browser.

When you visit a web page through a web browser, you can view the web page's HTML markup. In Internet Explorer, go to the View menu and then choose the Source option; in the Mozilla browser, click on the View menu and choose the Page Source menu option. This will display the web page's HTML content. To fully appreciate how complex this HTML markup can become, take a moment to visit Ford's website at www.ford.com. This website, shown in Figure B.2, is fairly simple looking, but the HTML required to display this page is daunting. Listing B.1 lists only a portion of the HTML markup for Ford's home page.

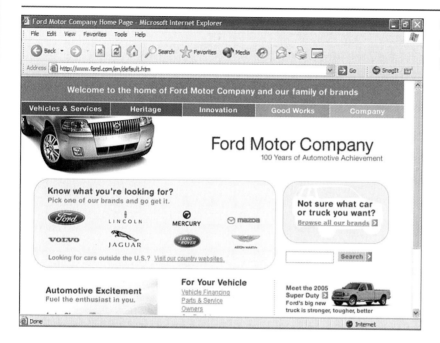

FIGURE B.2

Ford's website home page.

Listing B.1   A Portion of the HTML Markup for Ford's Home Page

```
<BODY bgcolor="#FFFFFF" text="#666666" link="#CC6600" alink="#CC6600"
vlink="#CC6600" topmargin="0" leftmargin="0"
marginwidth="0" marginheight="0">
<!-- Inserted by Content Management Server: BEGIN EmbedBodyBeginHook -->

<!-- Inserted by Content Management Server: END EmbedBodyBeginHook -->

    <DIV id="undecided">
       <TABLE border="0" cellpadding="0" cellspacing="0" width="200"  >
          <TR>
             <TD class="greyHome" valign="top">
<A href="/en/vehicles/vehicleShowroom/default.htm?referrer=home">
Browse all our brands</A> 
<A href="/en/vehicles/vehicleShowroom/default.htm?referrer=home">
<IMG src="/NR/fordcom/images/en/global/go.gif" width="12" height="13"
border="0" alt="Go" align="top"></A></TD>
          </TR>
       </TABLE>
    </DIV>


       <TABLE border="0" cellpadding="0" cellspacing="0" width="760">
```

Listing B.1   Continued

```
    <TR bgcolor="#CC4400"><TD height="14">
    <IMG src="/NR/fordcom/images/en/global/nothing.gif" border="0"
    width="1" height="1" alt=""></TD></TR>
    <TR bgcolor="#CC4400">
        <TD align="center"><IMG src="/NR/fordcom/images/en/home/welcome.gif"
        border="0" width="585" height="20" alt="Welcome to ford.com"></TD>
    </TR>
    <TR bgcolor="#CC4400"><TD height="12">
    <IMG src="/NR/fordcom/images/en/global/nothing.gif" border="0" width="1"
    height="1" alt=""></TD></TR>
</TABLE>
<TABLE border="0" cellpadding="0" cellspacing="0" width="760">
<TR>
    <TD valign="top">
    <A href="/en/heritage/centennial/default.htm?referrer=home">
    <IMG src="/NR/fordcom/images/en/home/centennial.jpg" border="0"
    width="174" height="189" alt="100th Anniversary"></A></TD>
    <TD valign="top"><IMG src="/NR/fordcom/images/en/home/henry_ford.jpg"
     border="0" width="108" height="189" alt="Henry Ford"></TD>
    <TD><IMG src="/NR/fordcom/images/en/global/nothing.gif" border="0"
     width="40" height="1" alt=""></TD>
    <TD valign="top"><TABLE cellSpacing=0 cellPadding=0 width=165 border=0>
<TBODY>
<TR>
<TD vAlign=top><IMG height=18 alt="For Your Vehicle"
src="/NR/rdonlyres//for_your_vehicle.gif" width=165 border=0></TD></TR>
<TR>
<TD class=greyText vAlign=top>
<A href="/NR/Financing.html">Vehicle Financing</A></TD></TR>
<TR>
...
```

This HTML markup represents only 15% of the entire HTML markup for Ford's home page! Clearly, having to write the HTML markup for a web page by hand is not an easy task. With tools like Composer, you can specify the formatting and appearance of a web page just like you would with a word processor such as Microsoft Word. When you create or modify a web page with Composer, it automatically generates the HTML for you based on the text, images, and formatting you add to the page.

NOTE

If you are interested in learning the actual markup language of web pages—HTML—consider picking up a copy of *Sams Teach Yourself HTML & XHTML in 24 Hours.* (ISBN 0-672-32520-9)

Understanding How the Internet Works

In Chapter 2, you learned the steps necessary for making the web pages you create accessible to anyone with a connection to the Internet. Recall that you need to host your site with a website host, which will make your website content available on a computer that has a direct and persistent connection to the Internet.

While Chapter 2 covered the steps you need to take to get started publishing your website content, it didn't delve into the specifics of how a web host provider makes your website available to all. Nor did it examine the sequence of steps that happen when a visitor enters your website's URL into their browser. This Bonus Chapter explores these areas. With a deeper understanding of how the Internet works, you'll not only better understand *why* you need a web host provider to create a publicly accessible website, but you'll also be able to impress all of your friends and family with your knowledge on this topic!

The secret to understanding how the Internet functions is to realize that the Internet is a lot like the U.S. postal service. In the next two sections, you'll see how the postal service works and how the Internet's functionality mirrors the postal service's.

Examining How the Postal Service Works

The U.S. postal service allows individuals to send a piece of mail to any address in the world. In order to send a piece of mail, you must do two things:

1. Specify the address to which the mail is to be sent.

2. Drop off the mail at a post office or in a mailbox.

Imagine that you want to send a postcard from your vacation in San Diego, California back to your friend in Albany, New York. You'd first need to write the address of your friend on the postcard: Let's say it's 123 Elm Street, Albany, NY. Then, you drop the postcard in a mailbox.

Sometime later that day, a postal employee will drop by the mailbox, pick up the postcard, and take it back to the post office. Your postcard will get sorted with other incoming mail, and will be placed in a box with other mail that's addressed to residents east of California.

The next day a mail truck would take the letter from the San Diego post office up north to the Los Angeles post office. There, the letter might travel by plane to the post office in New York City, New York. From there, a postal truck will take the postcard up to the Albany post office. Finally, a postal employee in the Albany post office will deliver the mail to your friend's home.

As shown in Figure B.3, the delivery of mail from San Diego to Albany travels through a number of post offices. What is important to realize is that oftentimes a letter passes through many post offices before reaching its final recipient.

FIGURE B.3

Mail travels through many post offices on its way to Albany.

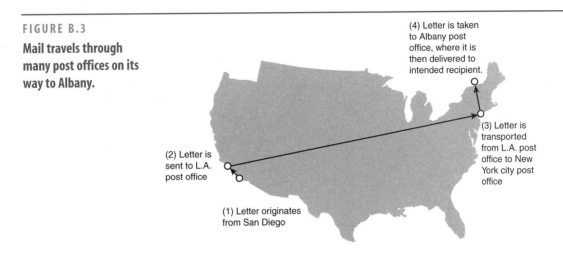

(4) Letter is taken to Albany post office, where it is then delivered to intended recipient.

(3) Letter is transported from L.A. post office to New York city post office

(2) Letter is sent to L.A. post office

(1) Letter originates from San Diego

In summary, the U.S. postal service has post offices all around the world. A piece of mail is delivered by the sender dropping off an addressed piece of mail to one of these post offices. The piece of mail is then routed through various post offices and finally is delivered directly to the addressed recipient.

The Internet as a Virtual Postal Service

The Internet is set up in a similar fashion to the U.S. postal service. The post office can only deliver mail to locations that have a unique address. For postal mail, the address is usually a combination of country, zip code, state or province, street address, and possibly an apartment or suite number. Computers on the Internet are uniquely identified by an *IP address*.

Recall that the postal service has post offices established around the globe to route mail across this planet as needed. The Internet analogy to post offices is *routers*. Routers are specialized computers that do nothing but route Internet traffic from an initial sender to a final receiver. In traversing the Internet, data might travel through upward of 20 routers before reaching its final destination.

Figure B.4 depicts the path a web page might take when being sent from a web server in San Diego with IP address 134.56.100.76 to your personal computer in Washington D.C. with IP address 87.213.20.119. Note the similarities between Figures B.3 and B.4.

NOTE

An *IP address* is a series of four numbers, where each number is between 0 and 255. An example of an IP address is 45.102.3.211. The *IP* in IP address stands for Internet Protocol, which, among other things, specifies how computers are addressed on the Internet.

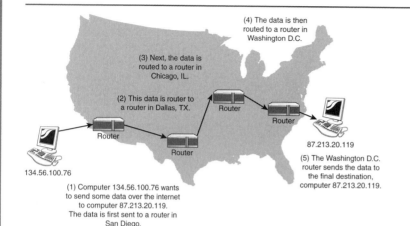

Internet traffic travels through routers in its trip from sender to receiver.

NOTE

The *domain name system*, or DNS, is a very big telephone book-like listing. In this big telephone book are the names of all registered domain names. Next to each domain name is the IP address associated with the website's web server. When you type in a domain name into your web browser's Address window, your browser first looks up the IP address of the domain name in that big telephone book. Once it finds the IP address, it then makes its request to the web server.

This big telephone book listing that maps domain names to IP addresses is maintained on a number of servers across the Internet. These servers are known as *DNS servers*. When a computer is first configured to access the Internet, one step includes specifying the IP address for the DNS server to use to look up the IP addresses for domain names.

What About Domain Names?

In Chapter 1, "Creating Your First Web Page," we discussed that a website is uniquely identified by a *domain name*, which looks something like www.someName.com, or www.someOtherName.org. However, just a few paragraphs ago I said that computers on the Internet are addressed by an IP address, which has the form XXX.XXX.XXX.XXX, where XXX is a number between 0 and 255. You might rightfully be wondering what relationship there is between domain names and IP addresses.

Recall from Chapter 1 that a website is a collection of web pages that are hosted on a *web server*. A web server is an Internet-connected computer that does nothing other than wait to serve up web pages to requesting web browsers. Since the web server is connected to the Internet, it must be uniquely identified by some IP address.

In fact, you can visit a website by typing in its web server's IP address into your browser's Address bar. For example, I can visit the website of my alma mater—the University of Missouri–Rolla—by either typing in the domain name—www.umr.edu—or its associated IP address—131.151.35.19. Figures B.5 and B.6 illustrate that using either the domain name or the IP address takes me to the same website.

FIGURE B.5

The UMR website, visited by entering its domain name.

Now, imagine that the only way to access a website was by entering in its IP address. Do you think you could remember the IP address for more than just one or two websites? If you called your parents on the phone and wanted to tell them about the new family website you and your wife were starting, do you think your parents would remember the website IP address if you said, "Just visit 64.123.99.7?"

The IP addressing system was designed with computers in mind. Computers work very well with numbers. Humans, however, remember words and phrases much better. Therefore, to make website addresses more memorable, a *domain name system* was established.

Figure B.7 shows the sequence of steps your web browser actually goes through when you type in the domain name of a website into the Address bar.

FIGURE B.6

Visiting the UMR website by IP address.

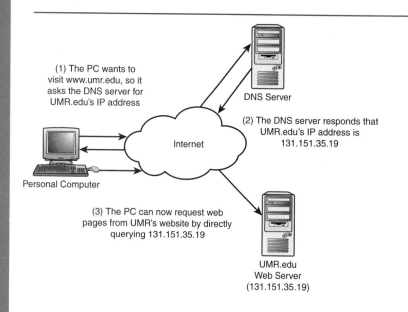

(1) The PC wants to visit www.umr.edu, so it asks the DNS server for UMR.edu's IP address

DNS Server

(2) The DNS server responds that UMR.edu's IP address is 131.151.35.19

Internet

Personal Computer

(3) The PC can now request web pages from UMR's website by directly querying 131.151.35.19

UMR.edu
Web Server
(131.151.35.19)

FIGURE B.7

A DNS server is consulted to discover the IP address for a given domain name.

Armed with a better understanding of how the Internet works, hopefully it is becoming more clear as to what steps are needed to create a public website, and why. In order to have others be able to view your web pages from their computers, you need to copy your web pages to a computer that has a persistent connection to the Internet. This is done by finding a *web host provider*, a company that offers such services. Next, you'll probably want to create a domain name for the site, which, as we saw in Chapter 2, can be accomplished by leasing a domain name with any domain name registrar, such as Network Solutions. When registering the domain name you'll need to configure the domain name to point to your web server. Finally, you need to upload your web pages from your computer to the web server.

This concludes the examination of how the Internet works. The next section in the Bonus Chapter examines how to optimize the digital pictures you place on your website.

Optimizing Your Digital Pictures

In Chapter 3, "Creating a Family/Personal Website," you learned how to customize the website templates by adding your own digital images. With today's technology, adding a digital image is as simple as taking a picture with a digital camera, or scanning a printed image with a scanner. In either case, the resulting digital image may not be ideal—it may be too wide or too tall, or it might be a very large file, which will increase the amount of time it takes for your visitors to load up one of your web pages. Fortunately, optimizing your digital images is relatively straightforward, as you'll see in this section.

When talking about digital images there are a couple of units of measurement that are essential to understand:

> ► The image's file size
> ► The image's width and height

Like any file in a computer, a digital image has a *file size*. The file size specifies how much space the image takes up on the computer's hard drive.

In addition to its file size, a digital image has a certain width and height. For digital images, the width and height are measured in a unit called *pixels* rather than in inches or centimeters. There is no direct translation from pixels to inches, or vice versa. This is because a given image's height and width in inches varies on the computer monitor being used to view the image. That is, even though an image might be 200 pixels wide by 150 pixels high, one person's computer monitor might show the image as 3 inches by 2 inches, while another's might show the same image as 3.5 inches by 2.75 inches.

"Since the computer's physical dimensions and resolution can differ from monitor to monitor, there's no universal translation from pixels to inches or the other way around."

This discrepancy is due to a number of factors. First, monitors vary in height and width from one another. For example, my laptop screen is 15" wide and 14" high, while my desktop computer's monitor is 17" wide by 17" high. Furthermore, monitors can run at different *resolutions*.

NOTE

A computer monitor's *resolution* indicates how many pixels are displayed horizontally and vertically. Common resolutions are 640x400, 800x600, 1024x768, 1280x1024, and 1600x1200.

TIP

An image's file size and width and height are correlated. That is, images with a smaller width and height typically have a smaller file size. Therefore, by making your images less wide and tall, you'll be making the file's image size less too, which will decrease the amount of time it takes your visitors to download your images.

Since the computer's physical dimensions and resolution can differ from monitor to monitor, there's no universal translation from pixels to inches or the other way around.

When displaying digital images online, both the image's file size and height and width can impact the user's viewing experience. Digital images with a large file size can take an extraordinarily long time to download, especially over slower dial-up connections to the Internet. Therefore, if your website has numerous large digital images shown on a particular page, it may take tens of seconds, if not minutes, for users to be able to view all of the pictures.

The image's height and width are important too. If the image is larger than 640 pixels wide by 400 pixels high, for users whose monitors are at the 640x400 resolution, the image will be larger than the browser window, meaning they'll have to scroll vertically or horizontally to view all parts of the image. Also, if you are displaying many images in a page in a storyboard-like format, exceptionally wide or tall images can make the web page look crowded and hard to read and enjoy.

Resizing Digital Images

Depending on the quality of digital camera you own, the digital images saved by the camera might be quite large in both their height and width and their file size. More often than not, you'll want to resize these images so that they're smaller both in file size and in their dimensions.

There are a number of software tools that can be used to resize a digital image. If you own a digital camera, chances are it came with such a program. If you do not own a digital camera, or if your camera did not come with such software, you can either download the appropriate software or use online tools to resize images.

FIGURE B.8

A picture of Sam (taken with a digital camera).

Let's take a look at resizing an image using the image resize tool at http://eee.uci.edu/toolbox/imageresize/. Figure B.8 shows a digital image I took of my dog Sam. The digital camera saves the photo at a rather high resolution—1152 pixels wide and 864 pixels high. Also the image clocks in at over 360 *kilobytes*.

Let's look at how to resize this image to a more acceptable height and width. Start by visiting http://eee.uci.edu/toolbox/imageresize/ in your browser. This web page, shown in Figure B.9, prompts you to select an image to upload for resizing.

Click the Browse button to select a file from your computer's hard drive. Once you have chosen the file to resize, click the Upload Image button.

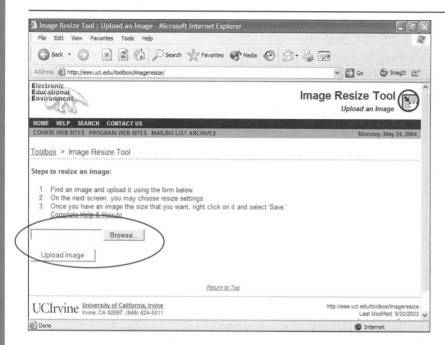

FIGURE B.9

The Image Resize tool helps you resize your digital images.

Once you have uploaded the image, you will be taken to a page that displays the uploaded image, its dimensions, and its file size. You are then prompted to select how to resize the image. You can reduce its size either by a specified percentage, or by entering in an absolute width and height in pixels. I am going to opt to resize the picture of Sam down to 320 pixels wide. After typing in 320 into the Width textbox, the Height textbox automatically is filled in with the value 240. This is the recommended height in pixels to maintain the image's *aspect ratio*.

NEW TERM

The *aspect ratio* is the ratio of the width to the height of the image. When resizing images it is wise to maintain the aspect ratio. If you don't, the image will look squished, as its resized width and height will not be proportional to its original width and height.

Figure B.10 contains a screenshot of the browser after entering the desired resize width of 320 pixels.

The image will be resized to 320x240.

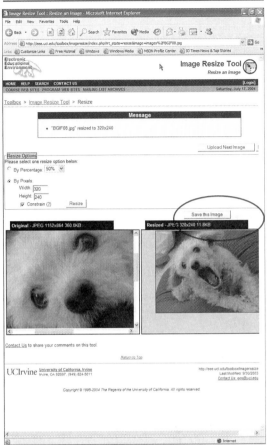

The resized image is shown alongside the original.

The last step is to click the Resize button. Doing so will display the resized image alongside the original, as shown in Figure B.11. Note that the resized image's file size is a mere 11.8KB compared to the original's 360KB! This resized image will only take a dial-up user two seconds to download, as compared to 50 or more for the original.

The last step is to save the resized image. To do this, either click on the Save this Image button or right-click on the resized image and choose Save Picture As. In either case, you will be prompted for the file's name and location.

When you plan on displaying digital images from your digital camera or scanner on your website, be sure to take a few minutes to first optimize these images. It will make your site look better to have properly sized images, and will improve your visitor's experience by decreasing the time it takes for them to fully download your web pages.

Summary

This Bonus Chapter presented a number of periphery topics that, while germane, were left out of the book's text in order to present more streamlined chapters. The Bonus Chapter provided in-depth information on the fundamental underpinnings of both web pages and the Internet.

In this Bonus Chapter, you learned that web pages are, in fact, composed of a markup language called *HTML*—while editors like Composer make creating and editing web pages a breeze, under the covers they are really creating and editing HTML documents. You also learned about how the Internet works, how each computer on the Internet is assigned an *IP address*, and how *routers* on the Internet direct traffic much like post offices do with mail. Additionally, the Internet contains a number of *DNS servers*, which provide a mapping from *domain names* to IP addresses. These DNS servers allow you to associate a domain name, like www.msn.com, with an IP address.

The Bonus Chapter also examined various techniques for optimizing your digital images. If you plan on displaying digital images you took with a digital camera, or ones that you created by using a scanner, it behooves you to first optimize these images to ensure that they have ideal dimensions and file size. By optimizing your images you ensure your visitors will have a more enjoyable experience at your website.

Index

CREATE YOUR OWN WEBSITE USING WHAT YOU ALREADY KNOW

U-V